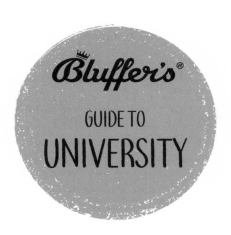

Bluffer's®

GUIDE TO
UNIVERSITY

D1307763

EMMA SMITH AND ROB AINSLEY

© Haynes Publishing 2019
First published 1988
This edition published July 2019

A CIP Catalogue record for this book
is available from the British Library.

ISBN: 978 1 78521 585 8 (print)
ISBN: 978 1 78521 632 9 (eBook)

Library of Congress control no. 2019934645

Published by Haynes Publishing,
Sparkford, Yeovil, Somerset BA22 7JJ
Tel: 01963 440635
Int. tel: +44 1963 440635
Website: www.haynes.com

Printed in Malaysia.

Bluffer's Guide®, Bluffer's® and Bluff Your Way®
are registered trademarks.

Series Editor: David Allsop.

CONTENTS

The Game of Life   5

First Things First   9

A Foot in the Door   23

Mind the Gap   33

Money Matters   39

Early Days   49

Survival Basics   61

Social Studies   67

Domestic Science   77

It's All Academic   87

Further Education, Minimum Work   103

Work-Life Balance   113

Glossary   124

It's all too easy to fritter away these years struggling to write essays, successfully spinning debt into credit or unsuccessfully spinning your washing.

THE GAME OF LIFE

University is a bluffer's paradise: interest-free overdrafts, optional workload, endless holidays, elastic deadlines, cheap travel and discount drinks. Even French civil servants don't have it this good.

As such, it is in among the gleaming spires, red brick and poured concrete of university towns that you will encounter the best and brightest of bluffers. It's tough competition. But if you can make it here, you'll make it anywhere (maximum points if you can slip that last sentence past a film studies student, especially one from York).

Although it's a struggle to get kicked out of university (you're only let out early on very bad behaviour), it is relatively easy to wander out of a lecture and never return. Even *Harry Potter* actress Emma Watson (aka renowned swot Hermione Granger) is said to have abandoned her undergraduate degree at the USA's Brown University. Admittedly, this was not so much a case of giving up, as of not being allowed to grow up. It was rumoured that Watson left after her fellow students refused to stop heckling, 'Five points to Gryffindor!' whenever she answered a question. At least this is proof that higher education produces more intelligent bullying, which is probably why Oxbridge produces so many prime ministers.

If you do make it to graduation there is no guarantee that you'll have done so in true student style. It's all too easy to fritter away these years struggling to write essays, successfully spinning debt into credit or unsuccessfully spinning your washing. And contrary to popular belief, this is not how you should be spending 'the best years of your life', as disenchanted former students tend to call them.

Instead, you should be feathering your nest with outrageous anecdotes, meeting people who you refuse to recognise as your social doppelgänger and neglecting to wash your sheets.

Luckily for you, this reassuringly short guide promises to let you in on the secret of MIMO ('minimum input, maximum output'; maximum points if you can slip that past a computing student as if it were a genuine computing term). It will conduct you safely through the main danger zones encountered in discussions about university life, and equip you with a vocabulary and evasive technique that will minimise the risk of being rumbled as a bluffer; it might even allow you to be accepted as a worldly student of rare knowledge and experience. But it will do more; it will give you the tools to impress legions of marvelling listeners with your wisdom and insight – without anyone discovering that, until you read it, you probably didn't know the difference between a 'Geoff' (a first) and a 'Desmond' (a 2:2).

By the time you reach the glossary you will be more than able to ace the game of student life. And trust us, university is a game. Play it right and you can collect money just for passing 'Go', score 75 points for a well-placed three-letter word, and win big on a pair of twos. What are you waiting for? It's almost lunchtime.

With a degree, you can end up with jobs you'd never have imagined yourself doing – working at a burger bar or a call centre, for instance.

FIRST THINGS FIRST

WHY GO TO UNIVERSITY ANYWAY?

How many undergraduates are currently studying at university in Britain? Depending on the time of day, the answer's probably no more than 2% of them. The other 98% are doing what students have done ever since Bologna started off the whole university thing in 1088: conducting research into chemistry and human biology of the decidedly non-academic kind.

In total, there are about 1.8 million undergraduate students, and half a million graduate students, enrolled at British universities. Why should you join the half a million people who start a degree course every year?

The standard reason is that graduates earn more. A man with a degree earns over £160,000 more on average during his working life than a male non-graduate with similar A-level results. For women, the degree dividend over female non-grads is even greater: £250,000. This will be enough to persuade most parents, or to put woolly-minded non-graduates in their place. But as a critical thinker of tertiary-education calibre, you know it's not as simple as this – because that average is inflated by the high-earning medics and dentists who put away a third of a million more than their unqualified peers. For humanities graduates, the figure is only £50,000; for arts grads, £35,000.

Today, a degree will cost you three or four years of £9,000 a year just for tuition. Add in living costs and, even with that part-time restaurant job, you'll rack up an eye-watering debt of between £30,000 to £60,000 – which, with interest, will involve repaying more like £65,000 to £85,000 over the ensuing years. Even a media studies first-year can see that those figures don't add up for everyone.

Of course, there are other benefits to having a degree, but even these must be taken with a pinch of salt. Graduates are fitter and healthier, for example, perhaps because they've slept a lot during the past three or four years and know about the dangers of a salty diet. (Though if being a graduate implies good health, being a student – with a lifestyle of late nights, junk food and excessive consumption – often doesn't.)

Research suggests that grads are also more active community participants – probably because they're going through their contacts book trying to get a job. They're also less likely to have criminal records, though that's possibly because they're smart enough not to get caught. They're more tolerant, too, on diversity and sexual matters, no doubt because they've done so much primary research on this themselves.

Bear in mind, though, that all the above figures

come from research done by postgrad students. So treat anything you read on their website with caution. Those PDFs may not be worth the paper they're written on.

But a university degree is about more than this. You make many new lifelong friends and contacts. And only a few new lifelong enemies. With a degree, you can end up with jobs you'd never have imagined yourself doing – working at a burger bar or a call centre, for instance.

You can learn not just about your subject, but about other people – and, most importantly, about yourself. People learn by making mistakes. So, in university, you'll learn more than you ever thought possible.

Best of all, for three or four glorious years you can overindulge, party every night, work as much or as little as you want, and somehow stave off all responsibility until you muddle through your degree at the end. And all on borrowed money. Yet everybody will think you're being worthy and sensible, investing in your future.

This book tells you how to bluff your way through with minimum effort and maximum effect. You can convince people that your ignorance is originality, your guesses are wisdom, your laziness is efficiency, and your random path through life is a well-focused grand plan – all skills which, far more than your 2:1 in English or engineering or sports studies, will set you up for the real world.

MATURE STUDENTS

If you're happy to join the post-A-level or post-gap-year stampede to uni with your cohort, fine.

If not, then starting a degree later on is a very good option. A quarter of students in the UK are 'mature'. Not a description of behaviour, but age; it means 'over 21 at time of starting'. Their numbers were rising steadily until increased tuition fees and funding cutbacks in access courses, which enable those without A-levels (or equivalent) to prepare for university. You can maintain that this is a government tactic to prevent those from poor backgrounds from studying politics and going on to challenge the status quo.

There are many advantages in being a mature student, principally that you don't have to act your age any more. Don't worry about 'not fitting in'; individuality is prized, so pass off your lack of tattoos or piercings, say, as a radical fashion statement.

Simply don't mention your age, or any event that happened before your fellow students' school prom. They won't be remotely interested in your past life – the world (or sex, which is the same thing) didn't start until they did A-levels. However, they'll be mildly impressed by your organisational and multitasking skills, perhaps honed from raising children or holding down an actual job: negotiating with authority figures, coping with hangovers, buying a round without having to visit a cashpoint first, being able to write longhand in joined-up writing. No hard-science university degree compares in complexity to filling in a tax return.

Tutors tend to treat mature students more as peers. There may well be an unspoken agreement between you: you're allowed to be late handing in if they're allowed to be late handing back. You're both grown-ups with other, serious, life commitments, such as family or (in increasing order of rowdiness) stag/hen/departmental parties.

WHICH COURSE?

There are something like 50,000 courses available for education beyond school. Picking the right one isn't going to be easy, but if you can work through such a complicated process, it prepares you for other even more complex life-challenges, such as choosing a mobile phone contract or energy tariff.

What people usually mean by going to university is a degree: a three- or four-year course in a subject or combination of subjects. It can be even longer if you choose to do something like veterinary science, dentistry, medicine or lots of resits.

Abridged versions of these degrees exist, perhaps involving only the first year (certificate or diploma of higher education) or first two (foundation degree). 'Sandwich courses' involve a year of paid work as a middle section of the degree, named after the structure – not the packed lunch which is the only thing you can afford.

Those studying languages usually spend their third year of four working in a country where one of their languages is primarily spoken, often as a teaching assistant helping locals who have poor English, such as the English teachers.

So which subject should you study? As in the job world, enthusiasm usually trumps ability. If you love a subject, you'll enjoy your degree. This is why geographers are always getting lost, mathematicians can't add, economists keep having to borrow money, sports studies people eat so many kebabs, and why those doing psychology have no idea about how people tick, so go on to lucrative careers in Human Resources.

SCIENCE V HUMANITIES V ARTS

Choose a subject to suit your personality. In sciences (physics, engineering, biology, etc.) you do tests to see if your ideas are right. In humanities (law, history, sociology, etc.) you see what other people have written to see if your ideas are right. In arts (art, theatre, dance, etc.) you just make everything up; being right isn't the point, it's being interesting.

No hard-science university degree compares in complexity to filling in a tax return.

Sciences tend to require more complexity-in-depth and cumulative study; arts a breadth and originality of viewpoint. You can't understand relativity without advanced maths, but you can write authoritatively about, say, twentieth-century art without ever having seen any Renaissance paintings (probably even without having seen any twentieth-century art either).

Whatever arts students will try to tell you, sciences are harder. But whatever science students tell you, arts are more enjoyable and your fellow students more attractive.

Finally, think of the financial arguments.

'Hard' research sciences and professions such as law, dentistry and medicine have the best employment prospects and higher ultimate earnings. (But competition to get in is very keen, too: about ten per place; five in the case of law.) So if money and status are more important than fun, go for these big-ticket courses.

Humanities – combinations of creativity and analysis such as languages, literature or music – offer enjoyable course content with some degree of financial return, though your most likely job at the end will be teaching humanities, which can feel rather circular.

Arts – creative disciplines such as, well, art – produce graduates who are barely more employable or better-paid than non-graduates. This is clearly the best option, offering very enjoyable courses with meagre financial return. So, because you'll never earn enough to reach the threshold to start paying back your student loan, you can have your three or four years of fun for free.

WHICH UNIVERSITY?

There are more than 500 higher education institutions in the UK. Finding the right one for you is like a student disco. It seems packed with possibilities; but the ones you'd like most are out of your league or taken by more eligible rivals, while the ones that want you are too immature, too scruffy or too desperate.

According to Wikipedia (from which you'll be cutting and pasting half your essays), there are at least 11 groups of university. It's easiest to think of these five, classified roughly by age (and decreasing order of prestige):

Ancient *(pre-1800: Oxford, Cambridge, St Andrews, etc.)*

Nineteenth century *(London, Durham, etc.)*

Red brick *(early 1900s civic universities: Manchester, Birmingham, Bristol, etc.)*

Plate glass *(1960s: East Anglia, Warwick, York, etc.)*

New universities *(post-1992 – former polytechnics or higher education colleges with names like metro stations: York St John, Oxford Brookes, Manchester Metropolitan, etc.)*

You should also know about **The Russell Group,** which is a kind of English Premier League of universities. Except that its 24 members selected themselves (initially at a meeting in London's Russell Hotel, hence the name) and there's no promotion or relegation to worry about. They consider themselves 'the best', and while many rivals contest that, they're certainly the best at getting funding: they hoover up three-quarters of all UK university research grant and contract income.

In a group of its own is the **Open University**, a popular and successful open-to-all, study-at-home option with 250,000 enrolled students. Established in

1968, it was familiar to TV audiences for its late-night lecture broadcasts until 2006.

OPEN DAYS

Matching yourself with a course and a university will involve a lot of tedious web surfing and possibly an open day. The latter is a valuable chance to see how reality compares with the university's web pages. Just because their website is well-organised, up-to-date, attractive and full of interesting content, it doesn't mean the place or the course will be. Or the tutors.

That said, most open days are well-organised and well-marketed. There'll be exciting, interactive presentations telling you all about your intended courses. You'll be shown images and videos of happy, culturally and ethnically diverse students all having great fun, and meticulously researched charts highlighting student satisfaction and rewarding post-graduate opportunities.

In fact, the open day may feel more like a presentation for a fast-food franchise opportunity than a degree course. But they have to be this way, in order to satisfy the most important customer: your parents. While you sit through presentations flicking through Instagram posts on your phone, they'll be grilling the academics on the most vital aspects of your intended course – probable future earnings.

Indeed, some unis have open days specifically for parents only. This is a good thing: encourage them to use it. Then they can have their day being convinced that fluid mechanics is a good maths option because of high-salary jobs in industry. Then you can have yours being convinced that fluid mechanics is a good maths option because you get to run barefoot across vats of custard, for viral films shot by media students.

MAKING THE CHOICE

The most desirable places to study for a degree are still Oxford or Cambridge, often referred to jointly as 'Oxbridge'. These two ancient universities each consist of numerous effectively self-contained colleges, many in historic buildings, as evidenced by the plumbing. Both are springboards for high achievers, which may supply you with amusing future anecdotes – for instance, how you're still waiting for the current chancellor of the exchequer to return the tenner you once lent them in the beer cellar.

Of the UK's 56 prime ministers from Walpole (King's, Cambridge) to Theresa May (St Hugh's, Oxford), Oxford has supplied 28, Cambridge 14, and other universities only three (including Gordon Brown, Edinburgh). Eleven did not go to university at all, including Jim Callaghan and John Major. You can use this information to prove pretty much anything about universities – or, indeed, politics.

Technically, the competition for Oxford and Cambridge is average: there are only five applicants per place (compared with nearly 14 applicants per place for the London School of Economics, or 'LSE'), though that's mainly because you need fistfuls of A-star A-levels, plus nonchalant extracurricular attainments, such as concert pianism and county-standard sport, to think about applying.

Oxford and Cambridge are world leaders in many academic disciplines, especially the most important one: chasing up well-heeled alumni for donations and bequests. Teaching students – with the lavishly uneconomic tutorial system of individual or pair sessions with tutors – is only the fourth most important Oxbridge priority. (The second is hosting conferences of American lawyers; the third is keeping the senior common room wine cellar stocked.)

Not making Oxbridge doesn't mean 'second best', though. You can easily justify your choice of university – however reluctant it might have been – by focusing on other factors. The reflected glory of famous graduates, for example: JK Rowling went to Exeter, where she was fined £50 for overdue library books. Or cherry-pick a metric from one of the many university guide websites ('I went for St George's, London, because it has a Graduate Prospects score of 94% on thecompleteuniversityguide. co.uk – Cambridge is only 87%, Oxford 85%!').

Here are a few more suggestions:

High entry standards
Some institutions can be pickier than the big names, so you're prouder of getting into Arts University, Bournemouth (entry standard score 161 in 2019) than York (159), for instance. (But beware of other bluffers who looked at the same website as you, and who spot that Cambridge scored 226, or Birkbeck London 95.)

The entry standard score literally sums up your A level results. Each A* grade scores 56 points, and each E grade 16, for instance. Top universities might demand a score of over 200 points, but what they expect is four A levels with mostly A*s, and not 13 grade Es.

Subject specialism

Nottingham is terrific for maths, Southampton is great for media studies, Liverpool for veterinary science – ha! Oxford doesn't even dare do media studies! A good one, this, as its plausible detail is hard to argue with. You can claim that your particular institution, whatever its reputation in other subjects, is a leader in yours.

Student happiness

What's the point in being successful and miserable? Buckingham and Aberystwyth score higher than Oxbridge for student satisfaction.

Cost of living

Inexpensive Cardiff or Canterbury are likely to leave you with more to spend on essentials such as alcohol (the second biggest expense for students according to NatWest, the first being rent), and treats such as books (the 12th). Pricey Westminster, Winchester and Bournemouth are likely to leave you with less.

Size

Manchester, with 40,000 students, is 30 times bigger than Plymouth College of Art. Oxbridge colleges feel small, too. Such everyone-knows-everyone intimacy can be a delight or a disaster, depending on whether you're trying to avoid someone you unwisely spent the night with.

Talking of which...

Male-female ratios

If you like being surrounded by women, put on your list Leeds Arts University (three women per man) or Stirling (two). If you're after men, go for Imperial College London or Loughborough (nearly two men per woman). Bear in mind that quantity is not necessarily an indicator of quality. (One 'best-looking student' league table put Loughborough at the top with Swansea, East Anglia and Leeds; the worst were Thames Valley, University for the Creative Arts and Bedfordshire. It's hard to find such information in these more sensitive times, which you can portray as either progress, or very sad.)

Staff-student ratios

If avoiding your tutors is a priority, go for a large student-staff ratio place such as the University of the West of Scotland (22 students per staff member) rather than St Andrews (12).

Other factors

There are plenty of 'league tables' available with even more niche factors, so you can always pick something obscure to justify your apparent choice. For instance, you chose Gloucestershire because it's green, or a London institution for its rainbow cosmopolitanism, or a distant province for uniformity. Or you chose Bolton, because its dropout rates are high – 30% compared with Cambridge's 1.4% – which means there'll never be a queue for the PCs.

Be wary of such online guides with too much student opinion though: like hostels on tripadvisor.com, simplistic ratings can be affected by rumours, grudges, and naive reviewers who have never actually experienced anywhere else, which is most of them. In practice, similar types of university will have very similar standards of teaching, similar course content, similar prestige of degree, and similar proportions of disaffected junior lecturers who leave for something more lucrative, such as delivering pizzas.

York, Warwick and Durham, for example, will have so little to choose between them – whatever the course – that you can happily select on factors particular to you. Perhaps you want to be near your family in Yorkshire, and choose York to be close to them, for instance. Or perhaps you don't want to be near your family in Cornwall, so choose Durham to be far away in the north. Or perhaps you love castles, beautiful English cities and Shakespeare, in which case don't choose Warwick. It's actually in Coventry. Always read the small print.

A FOOT IN THE DOOR

UCAS

Ucas – the Universities and Colleges Admissions Service – is the best way to enter higher education and get one of the half a million places up for grabs. Because, in the UK, it's the only way you can do it. It is pronounced 'youcass' with a sigh of things not yet finished, maybe not even started, and certainly not understood. There are no easy routes through Ucas; all are time-consuming and full of obstacles. Anyone who has tried driving to the University of Wales, Trinity Saint David, will know the feeling. The most popular involves applying while still at school or college with predicted, as opposed to obtained, grades. But because no maths PhD has yet come up with a formula for predicting the percentage of applicants who will fail to meet their offers, a lot of panicked rearranging takes place for these students once exam results have been released. Or, as Ucas calls it, 'clearing' and 'adjustment' (as in 'Venezuela's economy needs a little clearing and adjustment').

'Clearing' is like just making the last train home: you're in, but the best places have gone and you might end up by the toilet. You're in a pool of applicants trying to find a university (any university) and a course (any course) that will have you. Avoid this, especially if you suffer from low self-esteem. 'There's always clearing!' is one of the least cheering phrases to comfort exam-stressed friends with, especially if you suffer from high self-esteem. If you must mention the 'c' word, wait until after it's all over and then, depending on whom you're talking to, describe the process as a handy last-chance saloon or an apocalyptic bunfight.

'Adjustment', another example of dissembling jargon, is clearing in reverse. You only need know about this if you produce a surprise string of A*s instead of the Ds you were expecting.

Those who don't like counting chickens before they've hatched, whether doing agricultural studies or not, can apply as 'an individual' after getting their results. You can do this the year after sitting them or many, many years later.

Delaying the process is also useful because it gives you time to resit the exams you still have nightmares about. It's also a handy excuse to take a 'gap year' (*see* 'Mind the Gap', page 33). If you just want a sabbatical before re-entering education, tick the 'deferred entry' box. You can always tell parents who are wary about having you at home for another year that you did so 'accidentally'.

Whether applying while at school, or in between over-the-shoulder visits from your boss, there are a number of universal truths to consider:

1. It costs. A nominal fee of £12–£24, but a fee nonetheless.

2. You have to do some maths. Ucas has its own points system which assigns a different number of points to different qualifications. Courses will have a minimum points requirement, and the first test is working out if you meet it.

3. You can only apply to five universities and these can't include both Oxford and Cambridge. For those fortunate enough, braying about the 'problems' of deciding between the two is not a good idea, unless you don't mind being a guinea pig for dentistry students. Choosing just five may seem risky, but actually improves your odds. (In 2018, 37% of all 18-year-olds applied for university; 33% got a place.) The more applications universities receive, the more likely yours is to land in the admission tutor's 'overtime' or 'after-lunch' pile, aka the 'unsuccessful pile' or 'the bin'. Helpfully, Ucas defines the term 'unsuccessful' on its website: 'You have not been accepted by the university or college concerned.' Though if you need help deciphering this response, they probably made the right decision.

4. You have to write a personal statement (*see* below).

5. You need a glowing reference, obtained by whatever means possible. Although references are the last thing to be virtually paper-clipped to your online

application, they're the first thing you should organise, because annoyingly you aren't allowed to write, or read, your own. To avoid disappointment, target your referee a few weeks before the deadline with a campaign of flattery, not intimidation.

6. As with a tax return, census or flying Ryanair, Ucas imposes strict deadlines, and missing them will prove costly. The first one to meet is in mid-October. This is for those aiming high: Oxford, Cambridge, dentists, medics and vets. Mid-January is the deadline for everyone else – except art and design applicants, that is, who have until March, which is fashionably late. However tempting, try not to express the opinion that the later the deadline the less strenuous the course.

THE PERSONAL STATEMENT

This is often thought to be the hardest part of the application process – unless you're a mature student, in which case unearthing old exam certificates will prove to be the biggest challenge. (If you can't, and you're applying for archaeology, you may be trying for the wrong course.) But actually, your personal statement is capped at 4,000 characters. That's including spaces.

The fact that students are admitted partly on the basis of thin air reveals something about the whole university experience. Astronomy MScs can tell you that 96% of the world is made up of invisible stuff (technically, dark matter), so this starts to make a bit more sense. Philosophy students might cite Aristotle's adage, 'The whole is greater than the sum of its parts' – especially true when wondering why your round just cost so much. (Misusing facts and quotes like this is just the sort of thing you'll spend the next three or more years doing.) But writing even a thousand-odd words on your achievements to date can still be daunting, especially if you've achieved very little apart from some Instagram posts. Stick to the following rules and you'll be fine.

Remove all clichés from your first draft – though you may find there's nothing left. Your opening and closing sentences will most likely contain platitudes because you will be told and retold to make them memorable. Although you might imagine that these two sentences are all the admissions tutor will read (because sometimes this will be true), it is also important to remember that even Martin Luther King didn't open with 'I have a dream'. (He opened with 'I am happy to join with you today in what will go down in history as the greatest demonstration for freedom in the history of our nation' – maximum points if you can get that past a history student.)

Yes, keep it snappy, even err on the side of hyperbole, but do not Google 'good quotes personal statement', as this mainly produces lists of things not to say, and you might inadvertently use some of them. And whatever you do, don't mention your childhood. *The Daily Telegraph* found that a variation of, 'From an early age I have always been interested in...' was the most popular, and soporific, intro. It's an awful bluff; everybody knows advanced topiary was not your first passion, and that you were really just ruining flower beds and sitting in cardboard boxes.

Writing the bits in between your opening and closing statements is an exercise in damage limitation. There is always a way to spin string into gold, or at least into gold-plated string. For instance, if you dropped a subject (let's say critical thinking), don't say you did so to save your *joie de vivre*. Instead, explain that the structure of the course was limiting and you felt that your time was better spent organising a fun run/bake sale for Comic Relief. This lie works on multiple levels: nothing says 'mature individual' like charitableness and university tutors jump at any chance to knock the school curriculum.

If you're applying on your gap year, or on your third gap year, it is better to blame wanderlust than to admit that you missed the Ucas deadline three years in a row while distracted by home cooking and Sky Sports.

Luckily, very few universities still have the resources or the inclination to interview prospective students. Think of your personal statement as flat-pack furniture, not bespoke joinery: the contents can be chipboard and veneer, but just make sure all the screws are there.

INTERVIEWS

If you are called up for an interview, there are a few things you should do in preparation. Reread your personal statement. You'll want to reacquaint yourself with the ideas and opinions you now almost certainly don't agree with. It's surprising how easy it is to forget the sentences you spent so long agonising over. If you do end up arguing with your written alter ego, it's better to shake your head, laugh and say, 'It's amazing how much I've matured intellectually since I wrote that,' than to let your interviewer draw the only other logical conclusion: your personal statement was largely cut and pasted from the web.

It's also advisable to have turned your lies into half-truths and your half-truths into reality. That said, if you've casually mentioned EH Gombrich's *The Story of Art*, don't bother meticulously taking notes on all 688 of its wafer-thin pages. This will turn out to be the only book in the whole of the British Library that your interviewer has no interest in or, worse, no knowledge of. This is 'Sod's law', a more fundamental principle than even the laws of thermodynamics.

Don't dress like you're going to a funeral, nor to see Bruce Springsteen play Glastonbury.

Upon arrival, make a good first impression. Don't dress like you're going to a funeral, nor to see Bruce Springsteen play Glastonbury. Think comfortable-smart, as if visiting an elderly relative's birthday party where you have a chance of getting in the will. Personality is fine, maybe even a good thing, if you think that a mohican shows you're a free thinker. But remember that, more than anything, this interview is a compatibility test between you and someone rather older than you, who likes to think they've seen it all before. And almost certainly have.

As the interview progresses, the interviewer – impatient to get back to the sponge cake in the staff room – will mentally place you on a scale. Not of academic ability but of annoyance. 'Do I find this person tolerable?' they'll ask themselves as you claim that your earliest memory is of translating *Beowulf*. 'Could I converse with them every Monday morning with a hangover for three years between driving through traffic jams to get to campus and a damn departmental meeting?' If at any point during this half hour they decide they can't tolerate you, then you're out.

That isn't to say you'll only be judged on your drawl and the number of times you slip the word 'like' into each sentence. Sometimes interviewers will be interested in the answers to their questions, especially if they've asked, 'What effect on the whole of society does someone crashing into a lamp post have?' or, 'Can you write a formula that proves mathematics is interesting?' or, 'If a man speaks in a forest and there is no woman around to hear him, is he still wrong?' These curveball questions are, however, far less common than folklore would have you think, because academics are far less sadistic than they'd like you to think.

If you are faced with a fiendishly difficult question, this may sound paradoxical, but ask for help. Your interviewer, rather than assuming you didn't understand a word, will assume it's an astute interrogation of the question, a knowing request for analysis and clarification. Academics love showing off how much they know, and you'd be advised to encourage this. University is the one place in the world where you should let people you're not sleeping with finish your sentences.

And if all else fails, take heart: you're only as bad as your education. And university professors are the second-biggest critics of the UK's secondary teaching system (the first being the teachers themselves). They know that you've been taught pathetic fallacy and atom particle theory incorrectly. In fact, they know that almost everything you think you know is wrong and they aren't interested in testing you on your ability to repeat inaccurate information. (Unsurprisingly, they don't want their seminars to be full of students highly proficient in the art of parroting back Wikipedia.) Instead, they want to see how you think, which is perfect because bluffers have always been better at applied learning.

How many gap years? One before a degree is probably about right; and afterwards, about 20 to 30 while you wait for the recession to finish.

MIND THE GAP

The whole point about being a student is to have fun and avoid responsibility on someone else's money, while supposedly enhancing your CV. The gap year is a natural extension of that, whether between school and uni, or uni and gainful employment.

If anyone in a regular working job tried the gap year trick, subsequent potential employers would look on it badly. They'd refuse an interview, mainly out of envy. But as a student, you can easily pass it off as a way of 'gaining experience' and 'developing skills', when really you've just been on holiday.

Archetypal gap year activities might sound impressive – volunteering in a West African village school, running a diving centre in South East Asia, trekking in South America. You needn't be overawed, though; all these experiences have probably been bought rather than earned, fixed up at great expense through some agency that your Mum found online.

The money aspect can't be overestimated. In the previous millennium, when you were paid to be a student, you spent your gap year doing voluntary work (which you didn't get paid for) or some sort of job abroad (which you did). Now, when you pay extravagantly to be a student, you also pay to do gap year voluntary work, and even to do internships in remote countries. Or rather, your parents do, reluctant catalysts in the great CV arms race. If they're uneasy, a few references to hard-won success stories of, say, your friends' elder brothers and sisters, should persuade them: 'Ollie's sister paid to teach English in Beijing, and she's now on fifty grand helping businesses expand into the Chinese market. Emma's brother just worked at Burger King in his gap year, and now he's unemployed...', etc.

Everyone will know that 'duty manager at branch of multinational' means 'flipped burgers when manager was late'.

WORKING AT HOME

Any money you can save will help, most likely hoarded from a minimum-wage service job while living at home for a few months. Make sure you emerge with credible anecdotes of stupid-awkward customers, stomach-churning practical jokes by co-workers, and incompetent bosses, as evidence of your engagement with 'real life'.

You needn't dress this up too much for the CV. Everyone will know that 'duty manager at branch of multinational' means 'flipped burgers when manager was late'. Instead, use a vague term such as 'casual work at local restaurant' to explain those gaps on your CV which you actually spent watching daytime TV in your onesie.

WORKING ABROAD

You'll probably end up, like most people, paying an agency through the nose to fix up a few weeks rearranging shelves in a friendly but chaotic and undeveloped office or school somewhere remote, beyond even Google Street View (but still with live Premiership football).

If so, don't admit that you simply bought this CV-filler off the shelf. Imply you got it through 'local contacts', perhaps someone 'a cousin' met while travelling there.

Of course, on your CV, your experience sounds far grander than it actually was. 'Did status update for their Facebook page once' becomes 'social media editor'. 'Recharged school's laptop' becomes 'deputy IT manager and systems administrator'. 'Didn't understand my mild cultural faux pas even after 10 people tried to explain in broken English' becomes 'immersed in local culture with a wide range of people'.

Similarly, that evening you helped the warden wash up in Bangkok becomes 'temporary work as assistant hostel manager'. And the time you fed scraps to a dog at an Argentinian bus station is 'voluntary work on wildlife project in Pampas village'.

TRAVELLING

This is an essential. Your CV and, even more important, your Instagram and Twitter accounts, are incomplete without a tick list of places you've backpacked.

First comes the wish list. When telling people where you're going, choose obscure but cool countries; check Lonely Planet's online list of 'in' destinations, perhaps.

Look for a description along the lines of 'having got over its recent ethnic conflict/natural disaster/economic meltdown, the country is now being discovered by the savvy traveller for its amazing scenery/historical nuclear reactors/efficient body repatriation schemes'. The more unknown the country, the less likely it is anyone can challenge your apparent knowledge of the geography, language or illegal distilleries.

So, for instance, go for the undeveloped – Uganda rather than Morocco; Burma rather than India; or somewhere obscure and remote where few BBC journalists have ever dared go, such as northern England.

Talk up your trip before you go, then be 'gutted' when you have to pull out because of some last-minute visa hitch or civil war. You can then do your easy and enjoyable inter-rail round Western Europe, or your cheapo round-the-world flight via Bangkok, Sydney and San Francisco, in peace.

When relaying stories of your bog-standard backpacking trips, embellish them with the usual traveller's bluffs. Behind every amusing tale of mini-disaster – how you misread the Chinese characters for 'undertaker' as 'restaurant', for instance, or perhaps vice-versa – is the subtext that you were adventurous and resourceful enough to be there in the first place. (Maybe 'there' was only Chinatown in Manchester, but they don't need to know that.)

Everyone you met was either an 'amazing local' who knew all the cheap and unspoilt places to eat and drink and visit and invited you to stay in their house, or an 'incredible traveller' who wanted you to accompany them into Borneo rainforest villages or up unconquered Andean peaks. Look, here they are on your Instagram; that proves it.

And, of course, your trip will have been incredibly good value. Sneer at the millionaire's offspring who fly business class and stay in five-star spa resorts. Make up some just-plausible low figures for your incredibly cheap trip to India, northern South America or the central north-west of South East Asia: 20p bottles of beer, say, or £2 hotel rooms. And remember to claim that you were 'invited to be a wedding guest' by total strangers delighted to have Westerners in their marriage snaps.

HOW MANY GAP YEARS?

The more the better. One gap year before a degree is probably about right; and afterwards, about 20 to 30 while you wait for the recession to finish.

Tuition fees were trebled to £3,000 in 2006 and trebled again to £9,000 in 2012. It is important to remember that this is all Nick Clegg's fault.

MONEY MATTERS

LOANS

From the 1960s to the 1980s, university tuition was free. You even got paid for being a student; in 1980, students received a grant of £1,430 a year, which bought you around 3,000 pints of beer. Or a lot of books, but nobody ever did that. And you could claim benefits in the holidays.

Since 1989, though, when grants were frozen, successive governments have turned things around by stealth. A flat fee for tuition of £1,000 was introduced in 1998 and grants were replaced by loans. Tuition fees were trebled to £3,000 in 2006 and trebled again to £9,000 in 2012. It is important to remember that this is all Nick Clegg's fault (*see* 'Activists and Politics', page 73).

The trend towards the US model is clear. Columbia University in New York routinely tops lists of the most expensive university borrowed money can buy, with a year's tuition in 2018 costing up to $54,000 (about £40,000) – plus accommodation and living expenses. This explains how US student debt surpasses a trillion dollars – not far off the combined national debt of Greece and Spain.

You'll almost certainly have to rely on student loans to help pay your tuition fees and living expenses. You can borrow around £9,000 per year for each – in other words, over £50k for a three-year course. Even sociology undergrads can see that's an awful lot. But there's good news: your debt is written off 30 years after graduation. So, in fact, it's a 'student tax' rather than a 'loan'. The fact that successive governments managed to keep the black hole of such student 'loan' write-offs off the national balance books until 2018 is a lesson in bluffing for all accountancy students.

Tactics to help reduce your reliance on the loan include:

1. **part-time work** (in the same formula restaurant chains and dismal bars you'd otherwise be visiting anyway);

2. **choosing rich parents** (try not to openly exclaim, 'But Daddy says it's so much cheaper than Charterhouse'; pretend you, too, are living on borrowed money);

3. **doing a 'degree apprenticeship'** run by a number of well-known big firms or organisations (in which you're paid a wage to learn on the job, with your tuition fees paid too, and possibly a guaranteed full-time job at the end – but as you're employed four days a week and studying the other three, for up to five years, it's not an

easy or casually chosen option: at least by not having time to party, you'll be able to save up);

4. **studying in Scotland**, where tuition is free for residents. ('Foreign' English and Welsh residents get charged, punitively, up to £9,000 per year, so buying a flat outside Glasgow might work out to be cheaper. You'll have to prove you've genuinely lived in Scotland for three years beforehand, though, so it's not easy to pull this one off.)

Or, as a last resort:

5. **studying abroad**. Until Britain leaves the European Union, it's possible to study anywhere in the EU on the same basis as locals. So, in Germany, Sweden, Norway, Finland, Denmark, Poland, Hungary, Austria, Greece, Croatia or Slovenia, you can go to university for free. All you have to do is learn the language. Good luck following that lecture on Ricardian economics in Polish.

Applying for a fees and flat-rate maintenance loan is almost straightforward; if you can spell your own name you'll probably know the answers to the questions. Things get a little trickier if you opt to apply for a means-tested loan. Suddenly you'll need things like tax returns and patience. If still living at home, you'll also have to communicate with your parents in polysyllables as they'll need to 'support your application'. This mainly involves asking them to unearth financial documents and recall their login details (which they will refuse to remember receiving) so that you can complete the sections they started. Indeed, some mature students delay their application solely to bypass the need for parental 'support'.

If your application goes without a hitch, congratulations! This has been known to happen. But remember that Student Finance is run by people who understand your situation. Because they're totally confused by the whole system, too. Never take a loan calculation as final; it will be revised and re-revised and then returned back to the initially suggested sum.

If your bank balance looks suspiciously healthy and you realise that Student Finance has made a Monopoly-style bank error in your favour, don't rush out and buy a round of mojitos and a MacBook Pro. They always notice in the end and, yes, legally they are allowed to recall this money.

Opening a student bank account will also entitle you to an interest-free overdraft of perhaps £500–£1,000. Try not to think of it as free money; it will need to be repaid eventually and they'll have you over a barrel. The only way to beat the banks is not to owe them £2,000, but £2bn. Then, you've got them over a barrel. This worked for many companies in the late 2000s.

GRANTS

The saying, 'There's no such thing as a free lunch' – or, for scientists, the first law of thermodynamics – has two exceptions: maintenance grants and the 'five-finger discount'.

Maintenance grants are awarded by Student Finance and are always means-tested. So if your name's Minty or Sebastian you can skip this section. Privately run grant schemes, however – listed in a directory in your local library – are not always calculated according to your financial situation. Benefactors and boards have been known to place some very bizarre restrictions on their charitable nest eggs. For example, each year, the East Lothian Educational Trust awards grants to residents of the 'old' county of East Lothian, so if you live in Musselburgh, Wallyford or Whitecraig you're disqualified. The more specific the conditions, the less competition you'll face. This means that if you're the child of a Devonshire freemason, the £100 George Christopher Davie Masonic Scholarship has almost certainly got your name on it; and if a family member works, or used to work, at a post office in the south-west region, then the Horwill Memorial Scholarship is worth investigating.

Competition for grants is normally high, making mild larceny a useful fallback.

But competition for grants is normally high, making mild larceny a useful fallback. Coffee chains such as Starbucks do a great range of mugs that they rarely mind you borrowing (this is okay ethically because of allegations that they might have avoided paying some

UK taxes). Things like condiments can be borrowed from Wetherspoons (they're not real condiments, just things like them). For tea, coffee and cake make a note of the birthdays on your hall corridor and turn up at about four o'clock with a balloon, shouting: 'Happy Birthday! Charlotte's just behind me with your card!'

Alcohol is harder to get hold of, but your best bet will be attending evening talks, art shows or Eucharist services. Chlamydia test drives are always good for luminous key chains and condoms. You can often pick up free samples of toiletries, soft drinks and confectionery at major train stations during morning rush hour. With luck they're being dispensed by fellow students and you can fill your pockets.

This may all sound uncomfortably like actual larceny but it's an unavoidable and historic part of student life. In fact, the Latin motto *lorem mundus pusillus furtum*, dusted off for all ceremonies and fancy events, actually translates as: welcome to the world of petty kleptomania.

Alternatively, there's always the more legitimate student discount card. This carries a picture of you, far less attractive than you'd hoped – rather like the discounts you're promised.

WHAT TO BRING

Bed linen

White sheets are an awful idea because they show stains that aren't even there, but black sheets are a worse idea because they reveal how infrequently you plan on washing them. (NB: The more bed linen you bring, the less often you'll be forced to do laundry – those train trips home soon mount up.)

Bikes

Few people cycle at university: under 9%. Some unis are cycling havens – York is 23%, Cambridge well over 50% – but the closest most students get to a bike is when the Deliveroo rider brings their pizza. Yet bikes are perfect for student life: a cheap, low-maintenance way of getting round the campus avoiding lectures, or those bracing 7am rides home to bed. Bikes can usually be picked up for under a hundred quid from a local second-hand shop: cheaper and longer-lasting than your mobile phone, and less likely to be dropped down the toilet. Many unis provide route info, websites, cheap-bike schemes, decent parking and OK routes. Plus cheap or even free bike lights, an offer well worth taking up: when the clocks go back in autumn, weary local police will do a crackdown on students cycling without them. Promote the bike as the embodiment of modern student ideals. It's environmentally sound. It's been vegan for 130 years. It has no colonialist past. It helped emancipate women and the working class. It can be any colour you like. It might have an exotic cultural name you can't spell. And frame types, like gender, are non-binary: male, female, unisex, mixte, other, don't know. Most clinchingly, it's hated by a certain sort of white, middle-class, middle-aged man who pontificates against cyclists in the Lords or reactionary press. That'll get your fellow students on your side.

Books

Vital props for asserting your intelligence. *Catch-22, Ulysses, Infinite Jest* and a few Graham Greene novels should convince even the English students. Add margin notes, supplied by a well-read friend – 'cf Salinger', or 'yes, but see page 74', or 'example of anacoluthon'; or simply pick out some passages in highlighter. These suggest that you've studied and digested the texts, should anyone leaf through them.

Bottle opener, corkscrew

Essential for sociability, even if, like many students these days, you rarely drink. Cheap wine, ie most wine you'll encounter, is screw-top, but it makes a corkscrew even more of an prize possession when someone turns up with a corked bottle. In theory you can open a beer with a lighter, but in theory you can open a beer with your teeth. Doesn't mean it's advisable.

Condoms

A must, even if you don't have a need for them. Being without one would suggest that you don't have sex, which in turn suggests that you are not a student. Safe sex is also important (*see The Bluffer's Guide to Sex*).

Cushions

Not only a makeshift sofa, but also useful for mock fights with someone you fancy.

Fancy dress

Muster every accessory you can: wigs, frameless glasses,

neon fishnets, whatever's left of the school uniform you rashly burned on your last day of school, feather boas, ad infinitum. Diss anyone who rents fancy dress for parties. This shows a worrying lack of imagination.

Important documents
Folder for prominent display on the shelf to give air of organisation. Apart from your passport and driving licence, there's no need to be too discerning when compiling it, just as long as everything inside it is official-looking. Instruction manuals for electronic goods look vaguely impressive here.

Kitchenware
Don't worry too much over what to bring. After the first week, your forks and frying pans will be muddled up with the rest of your roommates'.

Laptop
A necessity. Pens, leather notebooks and beaten-up Penguin classics are only needed for posing.

Onesie
In essence an adult-sized romper suit; animal-themed is best. Important for refusing to grow up and accept a sense of social responsibility. Also useful for rag week (*see* page 126).

Plastic cups, straws
The former do away with washing up and the latter invite excited squeals from girls (and boys). Especially if they're

novelty-shaped. Becoming unpopular though because of environmental impact. You can excuse not having them because they 'take 5,000 years to decompose'.

Speakers
The louder the better. If they come with dials (which ideally they should), twiddle the bass up and down in a dissatisfied manner whenever somebody is looking. References to the volume dial in the cult film *Spinal Tap* which 'went up to 11' are obligatory.

Throws
Preferably brightly coloured and tie-dyed. Maintain these were bought in India, not Urban Outfitters.

Wall coverings
Blank walls signal that you are soulless, or at least yawningly dull. Boys: obtain a poster of either Che Guevara, Bob Dylan, or the 'Athena' tennis girl; egg cartons can make the room look like a Dr Who set very cheaply; avoid porn. Girls: collages made from the pages of magazines are acceptable (and cheap); arty postcards are perfect for proving your credentials as the next Charles Saatchi; or you can buy a blank canvas and throw paint at it to hint at some talent as an abstract artist. And everybody should display a few photos of dazzlingly beautiful friends from home, or who you met on holiday: never underestimate the power of suggestion.

EARLY DAYS

FRESHERS' WEEK

Your first week is officially reserved for finding your feet, though they won't touch the ground in this time. You'll be lucky if you remember your own name and what A-levels you did, never mind anyone else's. For the convenience of others, you'll be referred to collectively as 'freshers' (only once you've made it into your second year will you understand why this title, like forgotten milk at the back of your fridge, is so hard to shake). You will also be haunted by the sinister catcall, 'Down it, fresherrrr.'

The 'week' can actually last from three to 14 days, depending on the social credentials of your university. It consists of treasure trails, pub crawls, freshers' fairs and sourcing takeaways. These are advertised as a way to 'familiarise yourself with the place', but this is a ruse. Whether you've arrived to find a labyrinthine medieval city or Manchester's mile-long-straight of curry houses, it's sociability, not orientation, that you're being tested on.

You'll meet a million people, so finding a few you can

stand shouldn't be too hard. Err on the side of caution, though, and begin the week on a charm offensive. You don't get a second chance to make a first impression – unless of course you've spent the evening forging a friendship with somebody so drunk they can't remember you the next day, even though they claimed to be your best friend. Staying a bit more sober than everyone else is a useful skill to cultivate, though that's becoming a more finely-judged business now that students drink far less alcohol than of yore. Fancy dress parties are inevitable. As mentioned, home-made costumes, inventively acquired from charity shops, impress more than hired ones. Cross-dressing for men, especially rugby players, might be expected; 'Great legs!' is generally a safe compliment whatever the gender or sexuality. However, don't take the dressing-up too seriously in case you have to reintroduce yourself with each new costume – and you fail to live up to the promise of those legs.

Fresher's (bird/swine) flu is also a good idea to avoid, not because being bedridden with a hacking cough is unpleasant, but because you'll take yourself out of the social running.

If you do miss freshers' week, either because you've got a fever of 102°F or you're still looking for the launderette, here are the stereotypes you would have met and how to make up for lost time. (If you never meet one of these characters, it's because you're one of them.)

The Lad/Ladette
Easily identified because he or she will be constantly chanting: their location, what they're drinking, what

or whom they did last night... Although permanently inebriated, they'll have a useful social network. Arm yourself with enthusiastic high fives (to be dealt out whenever the conversation starts to wane) and come up with nicknames for everyone you meet.

The Player/Queen Bee

Unlike the Lad or Ladette they're too controlled to be seen out on the lash. They will have already picked up a dedicated posse of hangers-on. Don't act star-struck; it's mostly smoke and mirrors. Well, smoke, anyway.

The One Everyone Remembers from the Facebook Freshers' Group

Despite having added everybody on Facebook (often before arriving), they will go on to be as aloof as a heffalump. Keep contact virtual rather than actual for maximum success.

Tina Made Famous by Comedian Dylan Moran

Tina is the girl who leaves passive-aggressive notes in the kitchen, to which Moran imagined replying: 'Dear Tina, everyyyybody hates you.' A closed door will always come between you. Epistolary friendships only.

The Butterfly

Über cool, until their home-friends surface and unravel all of their hard work. To befriend, pander to their newfound sense of self (whether that be red lipstick and a penchant for vintage coats or a semi-permanent attachment to a pair of Sennheisers).

The Paparazzo

Their Facebook albums rewrite and determine social history, so make sure you feature by photobombing every one of their shots. Alternatively, comment prolifically when the photographs surface online.

The Londoner

You'll remember what London tube zone they live in before their name. In theory, you'll need an identical taste in music and social scenes to get along with them. But in practice, just keep them onside by criticising the comparatively poor nightlife outside of the capital. They may reference the various drugs they've tried; once again, you don't need to match this. The idea is not to outdo them but to bolster their own sense of hipster self-worth.

The Northerner

Constantly plays up to northern stereotypes and will preface any southern-centric conversation with, 'London, London, London…' Don't ever ask, 'Oh, are you cold?' Do mention the Midlands, as this proves you don't count everything above Oxford as 'up north'.

The Smoker

Resolutely combats the awkwardness of forced social interaction by lighting cigarette after cigarette. Not so much aloof, as constantly outside. Will invariably make friends with other smokers (or northerners) because of their shared understanding of what it means to be chilled to the bone. Conversations about the extortionate price of cigarettes and the best duty-free airports in the Far East are a sure-fire winner. If you'd prefer to keep your lungs intact but still want to move in these smoky circles, then adopt a rasping voice and nonchalantly say you swore off smoking after falling asleep with a lit fag in your hand and almost burning down the Vietnamese hostel you were staying in.

NETWORKING

As soon as you've established a group of friends (however superficial), you can afford to refine it. This is the only time in your life that it will be socially acceptable to abruptly stop speaking to somebody who, only a day earlier, was your best friend in the whole wide world but is today revealed as a loser. Make the most of it.

When deciding who to hold tight, listen out for mentions of holiday homes and vast family wealth. Both are useful for obvious reasons. But also make a note of what subject your new best friend does. Lawyers and medics will soon become so insular that, unless you find yourself in a murder case or serious traffic incident, they will forget what you look like. Beware linguists; they'll abandon you in your third year for a year drinking piña coladas and not getting caught in the rain. If you do befriend linguists plural, try to ensure that their common language is one you can also speak. Maths students are great for when it comes to the theory of splitting the bill but will get the amounts wrong. Scientists – used to testing by experiment rather than following general opinion – often have non-standard, non-cool tastes in music or humour but may have special access to distilling equipment. Anyone doing a subject with 'studies' in the title won't be doing much study, so will have plenty of time to socialise.

GOING OUT

Like nostalgia, university drinking culture isn't what it used to be. Yes, there'll be some rowdy rugby or netball club gatherings after the game, but student life these days will seem remarkably sober and focused to parents who remember the heady days of grants and 7/7 partying. You can speculate on the factors – financial or career pressure, wider diversity of students from non-boozing cultures, or availability of other substances – but the good news is it doesn't mean less fun. Or even more work, if you play things right.

One thing is certain: the weekend as you remember it, like your former life, is no more.

One thing is certain: the weekend as you remember it, like your former life, is no more. Your new schedule, of most nights in but some nights out, revolves around other factors, such as essay deadlines or sports practice. And, now and then, there will be those spectacular all-nighters that you talk about with your friends for years to come. (Trying to piece together what actually happened.)

Time dilation is a well-observed effect for students, and not just for those studying relativity. Being able to supply the hour of day, or indeed the day, will trigger suspicious looks from your time-addled friends. Never know the date, especially in any discussion of work deadlines. Unless it's the date your student loan is due to arrive.

Although cultivating a disinterest in the specifics of time, you should make a note of the five types of venue in which you'll let it slip through your fingers as smoothly as the money you just got from the cashpoint:

Pubs

Expensive. Even if you're not in a caring-profession course, develop nursing skills – the sort you do with a pint all evening. Spend your whole degree trying to find a pub that is just right. The spectrum ranges from the local Wetherspoons (sticky floors but great deals, such as breakfast that includes a free pint) all the way to the recently refurbished gastropub (which has acquired a Michelin star and elitist door policy since you last went there). Finding somewhere in between these two extremes (one has flowers in the toilet; the other has flowerbeds *for* toilets) is difficult, but throw yourself into it. The research isn't all that tedious.

Clubs

Although there are many club nights (and it's vital to know your night), roughly speaking, there are only two species of club: the garishly coloured paintbox variety with more sticky floors and neon drinks to match;

and its nemesis, the dingily lit underground venue where everybody drinks cans of beer but seems to have ingested something a little more mind-altering.

The first kind is very much geared to social interaction. The music is useful in that it gives you something to flail your arms around to, but knowing the song isn't essential. Nobody will notice if you don't recognise it (if only because you'll only ever hear the first 30 seconds before the hyperactive 'DJ' changes the track). Learn how to 'strawpedo' your Smirnoff Ice and you'll be the belle of the ball.

Just to be contrary, the second type of club is very much about the music, although to the untrained ear, one track will appear to span the entire evening. Luckily, it will also have few to no words so you can't embarrass yourself by forgetting them. What will attract unwanted attention is excessive levels of enthusiasm. If in doubt, talk scathingly about the rapidity with which songs are changed in the first kind of club and the popularisation of dubstep; claim to prefer techno. Mentioning electro is a semi-safe bet, but to real music fanatics this has come to mean 'the most mainstream pop you can imagine'.

Whichever club you choose, the kebab shop is life's great equaliser. It brings everyone down to earth. As well as bringing up the contents of their stomach.

House parties

Although not strictly 'going out' (especially because you can't leave your own house until gone 11pm), these often impromptu and always informal events will form an important part of your social life. The key things to remember are as follows: don't bring a cumbersome bag (you'll either end up clutching it all evening or stashing it somewhere 'safe' and losing it); hide your alcohol somewhere other than the fridge (far too obvious), or at least decant it into a rogue bottle labelled 'tonic wine' before you do so; and prepare at least three fail-safe song choices in case somebody tries to palm their DJ-ing responsibilities off on you.

House parties have an impressive tendency to return your fellow students to their fledgling states, so refer back to freshers' week stereotypes (*see* page 50). The only downside to house parties is that eventually you'll be pressured into playing host and you'll invariably lose your security deposit in the process.

Gigs

The trickiest thing about going to gigs is knowing the ones to get excited about and the ones to scoff at. Tread carefully; it's very hard to come back from a poorly received suggestion. The best litmus test is to Google the band, DJ or singer and then run through this list of questions: Did *NME* 'discover' them? Do acoustic YouTube covers significantly outnumber the original? Do articles about the band members eclipse news of their latest album? If you answer yes to any or all of these questions, then blacklist them.

If a Google search returns lots of remixes, this is a good sign, but if it returns no hits, this is an even better sign. You should then nonchalantly mention that you were introduced to said band/DJ/singer because your friend's boyfriend is or was a member. If the gig is positively received, you will automatically be cool by association; if it's not, you can say it all went wrong when your mate moved on.

Bars

No student goes to bars (apart from the union bar, which is nearly always full of naked dental students in upside-down drinking contests, and therefore best avoided). Bars are expensive, have inadequate seating and are full of yuppies and/or *TOWIE* lookalikes. Save this social scene for when you know the meaning of disposable income.

NOT GOING OUT

There are three kinds of not going out: staying in, 'staying in', and staying in for a few hours before you go out (aka pre-loading).

Staying in

Actually staying in will usually centre on communal viewings of classic films and trashy reality TV shows. These nights are a dream to host because people will come bearing packets of biscuits and mugs of tea which they will forget to take away with them (a little bit of washing up seems a fair price to pay for free snacks and crockery). They may even order a takeaway and forget to take all of that away as well.

But if you do offer up your room for the proceedings, bear in mind that different programmes will attract different audiences. Play it safe with *Game of Thrones* or a Scandinavian crime drama. As the host you will also be required to set up the home cinema, so ensure that you have working speakers, lots of comfy seating (this is where those floor cushions come in handy) and know Tina's Netflix password.

An impressive knowledge of indie cinema will also never harm your reputation. Know the classics (*The Godfather: Part II, Apocalypse Now, Pan's Labyrinth, The Shawshank Redemption*), the twentieth-century directors to name drop (Stanley Kubrick, Charlie Kaufman, the Coen Brothers), and a few cult classics (*Xanadu* – an odder *Starlight Express; Around the World* – the Beatles documentary; and *Ferris Bueller's Day Off* – classic John Hughes).

'Staying in'

The evening will begin innocently enough with a few friends watching TV or bemoaning last night's drinking and today's ensuing headache. Then one person will turn up with a beer, open it with an advert-worthy fizz, and the rest of the room, like sharks who have just smelled a drop of blood in the ocean, will flock to the feeding.

These impromptu gatherings are even worse to host than full-blown house parties. Primarily because no one will have come properly equipped, meaning that every liquid in your house, even the dregs sitting in the bottom of your old coffee cups, will be drained or downed.

Pre-loading

This is the name given to the part of the evening where you drink prior to going out – to drink. Pre-drinks will follow almost exactly the same pattern as 'staying in' but you won't feel shanghaied. Despite being organised events, the more casual your attitude towards the evening, the cooler you will appear. With that in mind, forget everything you may have learnt in Scouts, or through clichéd cultural references to Scouts: being prepared is not a good thing. That means don't arrange bowls of nibbles around your room, don't exclaim, 'That must be Nigel with the brie' every time there's a knock at the door, and don't worry if your glasses aren't actually glasses per se (mugs, plastic tumblers and jam jars are all fine).

SURVIVAL BASICS

PERSONAL SAFETY

If participating in a conversation about how to survive your university initiation relatively unscathed, you will assume an air of sagacity and point out the fundamental truth that it's never a good idea to get drunk in the company of people you don't know (at uni or anywhere else). Actually, it's never a good idea to get drunk with anyone in those first heady days of university, otherwise you might wake up in the wrong bed and regret it for the next three years. Next, stress the importance of never trying to find your way home unaccompanied late at night (inebriated or not). You might be arrested for traffic cone abuse. And, at the risk of stating the obvious, never take any pill or powder of a so-called 'recreational' nature (especially if it's offered by someone you've only just met).

DRUGS

Illegal drug use is no more associated with universities than the world outside, surveys suggest: half of students don't take them at all, and of those who do indulge on the campus, 80 per cent had started at school. And what drug use there is – laughing gas balloons at a party, for instance – can be portrayed as tame compared to 'real life' (which you can characterise as the desperate poor, in thrall to their dealers for cheap dangerous knock-offs; or as the loathsome rich, also in thrall to their dealers, for expensive high-quality stuff – either group, you say, being 'the real problem').

As in the entire world, cannabis is widespread at university. But resist the temptation to sound more experienced than you are about other drugs ('Yeah, nos is OK, but I'd never touch MDMA or K again...'); you'll be rumbled. Perhaps the best approach is to state firmly that you've never used any drugs, no no, and that you never would, but with an enigmatic smile. Then it's not clear if you're being honest, or are simply not letting on, but either way it sounds like you're not subject to peer pressure.

MENTAL HEALTH

The multiple pressures of student lifestyle – financial, social and academic – can take their toll. Students reporting mental health problems have increased more than fivefold in the last decade. You can bluff about possible reasons behind this if the conversation seems light-hearted enough. (For example, cite 'increased reporting because there's less stigma', the 'general state of the economy', or 'pressures of social media on self-image': use acronyms such as FOMO, 'fear of missing out', or invent some.)

Universities all offer help to anyone struggling, as should you if one of your friends or even enemies is finding it hard to cope. (Many students are able to take exams separately from their peers, for instance, if they can demonstrate that the clearly unnatural stresses of a packed exam hall will adversely affect their mental state.)

Offering sympathy and support, at least, needs no bluffing techniques: what you have to do is listen. If you can offer this skill – one that's in surprisingly short supply – when someone really needs it, you'll have achieved more than any expert bluffer wangling a first.

ANTI SOCIAL MEDIA

The main threat to your security is the usual one – don't leave your phone unattended, especially if it isn't password-restricted. Otherwise, you may find Facebook, Twitter and Instagram posts appearing under your account that you certainly didn't write.

However, it's good to let people *think* you leave your phone unattended regularly with no password protection, so that you can explain away some of those posts that you actually did write, but wish you hadn't, by saying you were 'hacked'. Celebs get away with this all the time, so you should be able to.

POLITICAL CORRECTNESS

Reassure friends and relatives back home: dismiss all fevered press reports, and anything shared online, about 'student PC gone mad' or overly sensitive 'millennial snowflakes'. Those stories about statues of colonial oppressors being hauled down, or Shakespeare plays being removed from the reading list because of violence, racism and sexism, are wildly exaggerated clickbait. In practice (you tell your worried parents reassuringly) universities are just as chaotic, fearless and impassioned places for debate as ever, with all shades of opinion, some of them naive and unworldly, represented. And that's just the academics in departmental meetings, debating all-gender toilets.

Take 'trigger warnings' for instance – the idea that anything which could remotely offend, such as a rape scene in literature, needs prior advice and an opt-out for the overly sensitive. *The Guardian* found no example in any British university of any text removed from a reading list for PC reasons. Nor could it find serious examples of speakers being similarly 'no-platformed' – denied access to public debate.

In fact, the most pressing problems you'll likely find won't be political sensitivity, but the lack of women's toilet space. Old buildings typically have segregated male-female, which leads to queues outside the women's. Some new buildings have all their toilets any-gender, which leads to queues outside all of them. Others have a mix of male-only, and any-gender, which leads to arguments.

Take note of the following handy techniques for PC discussions:

* **Discredit the source.** (*'That website is a covert right/ left-wing propaganda tool illegally financed by American big business/Russia'*)
* **Counter-intuitive detail.** For instance, vegan food is actually exploitative (*'produced by slave labour in Indian pomegranate farms'*) and environmentally damaging (*'your avocado has more airmiles than you do'*). Give the source as *'something I read in* The Guardian/ Telegraph'.
* **Accusations of hypocrisy.** (*'It's a climate change conference – but they all flew there!' 'She claims to be a vegetarian – but they're leather shoes!'*) Hypocrisy is a particularly useful weapon, as it diverts attention from the central issue.
* **Equality of opportunity v Equality of outcome.** (*'Warehouse work is physically more demanding than manning the tills, so is paid more. Nothing's to stop girls from applying for such jobs, but they don't. Should we force equality of pay for clearly unequally desirable work? Force 50-50 gender balance for both roles? And simultaneously 50-50 for white and black people? etc*).
* **Quibbles with language.** See above. ('It's *'staffing'*, NOT 'manning', it's *'women'*, NOT 'girls', it's *'people of colour'*, NOT 'black people'...) Again, try to avoid being pinned down for a view on the matter being debated. Absolutely any term can be described as 'actually, that's really offensive'.

GENDER IDENTITY

Male, female, intersex, non-binary, trans, fluid, etc: with your enlightened 21st-century attitudes, you happily embrace everyone. Just try not to do it too literally at parties. Know what LGBTQI stands for (Lesbian, Gay, Bisexual, Transgender, Questioning/Queer, Intersex; check your student union literature, or Google for the most recent extensions, such as LGBTQQIA, or LGBTQIAPK+, or just make some up. And whatever you do, don't make the mistake of mentioning MGBGT (it's an iconic sports car of the 1960s and 70s).

In fact, don't get drawn into any discussions about definitions, or details of conflicting rights, such as male-to-female trans athletes competing in power events against cis-females (women born women; know your terms). You'll offend someone. Stick to criticising the imagined prejudices of some target group (readers of any given tabloid newspaper, elderly relatives, 'the 1970s', etc). Everyone will agree about that.

SOCIAL STUDIES

A CV consisting solely of academic and work achievements will not please employers. They'll be worried you'll want their job. Therefore, you need a list of extracurricular activities proving that you're a 'well-rounded person' – so well-rounded that employers can easily push you around.

But beware. Each activity comes with an attached social scene. Once in, it's hard to leave. Assimilation happens imperceptibly, by degrees; you'll audition for a play and do a bit of netball practice, and before you know it you're staying up till 5am to read lines with your co-star, before getting up at 6am to wash the team kit.

Here's all you need to know about social anthropology – in other words, groups and cliques. Most of them are like Japan, Ukraine and other countries that prohibit dual citizenship; they won't allow you to be a member of any others.

JOCKS AND SPORTS

Made infamous by films set in US high schools, the more jocks get themselves a bad name, the more they revel in it. Often the logical evolution of the Lad or Ladette (*see* 'Early Days', page 50).

Although seemingly identical, jocks are organised into a complicated hierarchy. Roughly speaking, there are mixed netballers, footballers and rugby players (all other sportsmen or women fit somewhere in the spectrum). While muscle definition and sporting status increase from left to right points of the spectrum, a tendency to intellectualise about sport dwindles. A rugby prop-forward is unlikely to use a phrase like 'tendency to intellectualise' and more likely to set light to their farts, for instance.

You could ingratiate yourself by trying out for a team (see the relevant *Bluffer's Guide*), but it's far easier to adopt the role of team social secretary, either formally or informally. This involves organising team practices, timetabling matches, masterminding socials and knowing the rules of the game, or at least the drinking games. When the season starts, feign a hamstring injury, and when the drinking ban comes into effect two weeks before the league final, go home for a fortnight. If you're asked to don a sweaty eighth-hand cat costume and prance around as the team mascot, you've been caught out. The aim is to be the social keystone of the team, albeit one that is temporarily crocked – not to channel the character of Mouth in *One Tree Hill*.

THESPS AND THE THEATRE

Student theatre is a great night out; the tickets are cheap and they let you drink through the performance. But discovering what's on might prove to be tricky because, due to the fact that most 'theatres' will only be able to accommodate friends and hangers-on of the cast, publicity is never a main priority. The beauty of this is that once you've made it into the audience, everyone will assume you're supposed to be there.

If the worst happens and someone has the temerity to question your bona fides, explain that you were down in London playing the entire female cast in an experimental performance of *Hamlet*. If they start to look suspicious, ask if they're going to the Fringe again this year and await a stupefyingly self-appraising monologue on the subject (the Fringe being the Edinburgh Fringe, a month-long theatre and comedy festival that takes place throughout August). Everybody will talk about taking their play to the Fringe, and some of them actually will. There's no real need to go yourself, although it is a lot of fun. Just mention C venues and the attached bar, the late lamented Forest Fringe, and lasagne sandwiches. If asked how you managed to find accommodation, in a period when prices quadruple and everywhere is full, talk vaguely about 'crashing on a friend's floor'.

Theatre people are split into two camps: the ones who just adore being on stage, darling (namely actors), and the ones who prefer the dimmer backstage lighting (namely everyone else: producers, stage managers, techies, set designers, make-up artists, etc.). Then there are directors who, in the Venn diagram of theatre, live in the overlap between these two circles.

Note that everyone is to be referred to by their proper industry title. Student theatre is a serious business and 'am dram' (amateur dramatics) is a dirty phrase. But mock all you want, now; these are the proactive aesthetes who'll be waltzing across living room TV screens in a few years' time. Befriend early on. Watch out for the Andrew Lloyd Webbers-in-training, who narrate their daily routine in song. If being woken up to a concerto on the importance of brushing your teeth sounds like fun, join in for the chorus. You'll have made a singing partner for life. Or at least until the divorce.

For a less chipper double act, search out the aspiring comedians. They're far better at poking fun at themselves and have been known to do quite well. Oxbridge has a strong track record in both comedians (Monty Python, Armando Iannucci, Stephen Fry, Mitchell and Webb, Armstrong and Miller, Mel and Sue et al – and, er, Mr Bean) and politicians (*see* 'The Game of Life', page 5), though the line between the two is increasingly blurred nowadays.

MUSOS AND MUSIC

Enjoying the music scene is a relatively easy thing to do (*see* 'Going Out', page 54). Gaining the trust and respect of music types is harder. With some, you gain respect by having a solid musical background – at least grade eight piano. With others, the reverse is true, and even minor prowess on the ukulele is treated as dangerously 'classical'. Meanwhile, traditional rock bands are being relegated to the realms of a distant past. These days, at university, you're more likely to find yourself living next door to a subpar Skrillex with a pair of cans and a deck than the reincarnated Kurt Cobain.

But don't let the plethora of DJs or the complex Lego construction of their record-playing machines defeat you, if that's the direction you want to take. The great thing about DJ-ing is that it's essentially plagiarism and there are numerous apps that promise to turn you into the love child of Mark Ronson and Calvin Harris. If even this sounds daunting, continue on to the second page of YouTube and you'll find a remix obscure enough to pass off as your own.

Any group that gets to go on 'tour' is contractually bound to have a fantastic time and come back with guilty gossip.

On another note (probably a slightly flat one), don't underestimate the choir. Any group that gets to go on 'tour', even if it is to sing hymns in churches, is contractually bound to have a fantastic time and come back with guilty gossip. However angelic their voices or pristine their robes, they did something silly out there. Luckily, they're dying to tell you; nothing that happens on tour stays on tour. Keep this secret even slightly more successfully than they managed to and you might just be trusted to join next year's trip (regardless of your faltering falsetto).

HACKS AND JOURNALISM

As with student theatre, student journalism is a perfect rip-off of its real-life equivalent. Deadlines are fraught, scoops are celebrated, and rivalries between different news outlets run deep (watch out for being fed false tip-offs by rival hacks).

It's very easy to get involved in student journalism, as every paper is constantly taking on new recruits. Mostly because you don't get paid anything (rather like real journalism these days, see *The Bluffer's Guide to Journalism*), but also because a term is about as long as anyone can cope with the extra deadlines. It's worthwhile getting involved, though, because pretending to be a writer, even for a term, looks great on your as-yet-unwritten CV. Two things to keep in mind are that every punning headline, however original or clever it seems, has been thought of before by either *The Sun* or *The Guardian,* or even Bluffers. com; and that the journalists who go on to succeed are the most ruthless, not necessarily the most talented. (In ten years' time when they're BBC correspondents, you can remark that when you were rewriting their illiterate stories, they were so dim they thought Pearl Harbor was a blues singer.)

Experimental and occasional publications abound. Some will claim to be magazines, but most will accept the status of 'zine' (not necessarily half as good as a magazine but always half as professional-looking). These zines will be thought up at the pub, often very late at night, and solely feature articles by the people who started them. To set one of these up, all you need is two to three vaguely literate friends, a one-word title (preferably something along the lines of *Heure, Gioventù,* or *Mots*) and a black-and-white printer (the more budget-looking the final publication, the more integrity you can claim to have – just look at *Private Eye*). If the costs associated with printing enough copies for the three contributing editors prove to be too much of an investment then you can always start a blog.

ACTIVISTS AND POLITICS

Nowadays, passing for a politically engaged individual is as easy as calling Tony Blair, or Boris Johnson, or Nigel Farage, or in fact any major political figure an incompetent, feckless liar. Sometimes it might even be true.

American students, who are paying even more than you, will have little sympathy, however, and will regard all politicians as 'European' and 'liberal' (both terms of abuse). Overseas students, who also pay big time, will have no sympathy either, but they'll be too busy working to bother you.

If you are determined to be the voice of reason, or

doom, remind your fellow students that the cost of university has been increasing steadily since 1998. Then, with a sigh worthy of Mother Teresa (maximum points for knowing she was Albanian, born Anjezë Gonxhe Bojaxhiu in Skopje), say, 'In ten years when they're paying £18,000 a year, they'll think we had it easy.' Thus you can appear aware, sympathetic and politicised with minimal effort.

That said, university is the best place for adopting an audacious political stance. There are just two rules to bear in mind: keep it radical and keep it left. If you're lucky, a student sit-in will take place while you're at university and you'll be able to test out your anarchistic dogma by breaking into university buildings and painting banners. These events are great fun and also provide the perfect excuse for not handing in that piece of coursework or attending the last eight weeks of lectures. But remember to locate a back door to slip through undetected when you want a shower or a meal that doesn't consist of Doritos.

Bluffers looking to go the extra mile should suss out the post of student union president early on. This involves befriending the current president and becoming their protégé. While resisting their demands to sleep with them (a valuable early lesson in separating sex from the workplace), run for 'office', winning the popularity contest off the back of the past president's friends and followers, and enjoy your fully funded year out. Organise some sort of protest against unpopular legislation, organise a sit-in, a boycott of lectures or a campaign of minor public mischief –

especially as the last two happen most of the time spontaneously anyway.

At some stage, while all or some of the aforementioned activities are taking place, you will be expected to attend lectures and tutorials and study for your chosen degree. Don't take this too seriously; it's entirely incidental to the more important business of getting an education.

If you can survive a year battling for fridge space and avoiding the Hoover and the washing-up, you can survive anything.

DOMESTIC SCIENCE

LIVING IN v LIVING OUT

You'll probably be living 'in hall' (in university-run halls of residence) for your first year. These may be a short walk or long bike ride from everywhere else. At most universities, though, for one or more of the subsequent years, you'll be 'living out' (finding your own place to live, probably a shared house a satnav distance away).

Living in hall means fixed, predictable costs for rent, utilities, and meals, which, if the hall is catered, will be provided (and prepaid) in a canteen. It's not cool. Living out means you're at the mercy of money-grabbing landlords, who are probably business graduates who can't make a living any other way. In spite of the lousy economics, it is much cooler.

Living out means your neighbours are a lottery. They could be quiet and friendly, or loud and antisocial. Living in is worse, though, because all of your neighbours are students.

Meals living in are cheap compared to living out, in theory, because of fixed costs and canteen prices. But not in practice, because you'll miss most of them, especially breakfasts after getting up late, and wind up visiting cafés or takeaways anyway.

Meals living out are cheap compared to living in, in theory, because you can meal-plan and buy efficiently. But not in practice, because you'll only eat with your housemates for the first two evenings, after which clashing schedules – and personalities – mean you'll end up visiting cafés or ordering takeaways.

It's easy to sound expert on buying cheap food locally. You know which supermarkets have the best bargains. (Aldi or Lidl, with their obscurely sourced brands, always sound a convincing choice. Make out you're familiar with the excellence of English mozzarella, Lithuanian chocolate, Romanian abattoirs, etc.) You also know where to get the most dramatic sell-by date markdowns before closing time (have stories about getting ten-quid joints of beef for 50p from Waitrose or similar).

You know which cheap own-brands to buy. They're made covertly by the big names in the same factory, with the same ingredients, but supplied on the cheap under different brands – cite the recent examples of someone finding a KP pack of Hula Hoops inside Aldi's own-brand 'Snackrite' multipack. Consult the forums of money-saving websites such as moneysavingexpert. com: they'll give you instant apparent expertise, even if you've still not got round to doing any shopping.

SETTING UP A SHARED HOUSE

The anarchic squalor of the 1980s BBC TV series *The Young Ones,* and the soap-like personal turmoils of the 2010s' *Fresh Meat,* are described as 'comedies' about life in a shared student house.

You know better. They're actually instructional videos. If you can survive a year battling for fridge space and avoiding the Hoover and the washing-up, you can survive anything.

Finding a house is straightforward; the union will have a network of contacts. Finding the people to share with won't be.

At first it'll seem easy. By the end of the first week you'll have assembled a cosy group of new best friends to cohabit with in that second year. Then two of them will sleep with each other. Then with someone else. Then fall out with each other. Then with you. Then you'll sleep with one of them. Then everyone will fall out with everyone else.

And the next week could be just as eventful. Things move fast in student life.

Your ideal list of housemates may have a very different look and feel at the end of the year than it did in the first week – as will the housemates themselves, following a year of parties, lie-ins, takeaways and terrible tattoos that seemed such a good idea at the time.

The best tactic is to not commit yourself to any specific house or group of people until you have to. Talk vaguely about a second-year contact who has a 'really good house' that they can hand over to you next year. Doubt about the number of bedrooms means you can't nail down exactly who will join you in this dream home. Stick simply to expressions of interest from your potential housemates, and keep the candidate list fluid.

Have plausible reasons to rule people out whom you don't like without offending them ('We'd love to have had her in the house, but she's like, really allergic to cats, and I'm sure there were, like, five of them in the house when we visited – really, really hairy ones…'). Similarly, have enticements for those you want to keep sweet ('There's a cool shed thing at the back; it'd be perfect for your bike…').

WHAT TO LOOK FOR IN A SHARED HOUSE

Clearly you'll need fibre-optic broadband Wi-Fi with unlimited download. Other people fritter it away watching YouTube videos and films on demand, but you use it wisely watching YouTube videos and films vital for your coursework.

You'll need a washing machine, too – preferably one with a 'quick' setting. Otherwise, it'll still be churning away when people have to leave for lectures, so you'll end up having to empty and hang out their clothes before you can use it. Make up some stat to justify everyone else using the quick wash ('*New Scientist*/moneysavingexpert.com said that 95% of the cleaning is done in the first 10 minutes,' etc.).

Obviously, you choose to use the standard long wash. That way, you get your clothes hung out for you while you're at the pub. Or tossed in the bath, which is really, like, uncool.

Consider the transport situation between your house and the university itself. A bicycle is almost certainly the answer to everything, including finances, fitness and mental well-being ('I'm not a smug cyclist. I'm just pleased because I'm superior to everyone else'). However, you can easily find excuses as to why you have to go by bus (sporting injury, delicate laptop, rain may damage coursework, etc.). Cycle maintenance is important: keep it dirty and muddy to give the impression of rugged, regular use.

Hints to parents about nervousness walking home at night may elicit some sort of bus/taxi/Uber grant. Or even a modest runabout.

At some point you'll have to interact with the landlord. Don't bother trying to convince them that you all love cleaning, don't know anyone who smokes, won't have parties and will redecorate it for free at the end, because they won't believe you. They've had students before, remember; that's what deposits are for. All they hope is that you pay up on time, don't trash the place, and return the keys when you go. Be very suspicious if they want to be your friend. That'll be because they haven't got any others – always a bad sign, and you might have them turning up on a Friday night 'wondering' if anything's 'happening'.

Establish some ground rules for guests – how many and how long you can invite them to stay. (Classic misunderstanding: 'Do you mind asking your mate to move on? He's been here two weeks.' 'My mate? I thought he was your mate!')

Not all houses will allow animals, whether or not

you need to experiment on them for your course. The same goes for smoking; if the house itself is smoke-free, decide your policy on smoking in the garden, bearing in mind that your neighbour might be a police officer, or drug dealer, or both.

If you can get a deal that includes bills, great, though you'll probably have to pay at least the non-fixed charges (electricity, gas, phone) yourself. 'Yourself' being the operative word if you haven't set up joint-name liability with your housemates. You might be able to encourage payment-dodgers with dark stories of former students (the older brother of a friend, say) being chased up a decade later with court actions that ruined their careers.

Everyone ignores cleaning rotas so there's little point in setting one up.

You may well be liable to pay for a TV licence. You don't need it to have a TV (if all you do is watch DVDs, for instance) but you do need it to watch any live broadcast TV, via aerial or online, whether BBC or not – yes, even that live stream of news from Venezuela. You also need it to watch anything, including catch-up, on BBC's iPlayer. It's hard to separate fact from fiction in the corpus of stories about dodgers being caught or getting away on technicalities (or, indeed, genuine non-TV owners being hounded by overzealous officials from the enforcers Capita), but scan the internet and take a pro- or anti-licence stand one way or the other. 'Detector vans' are effectively a myth, but threatening letters and visits from Capita officials who peer through your window at your TV are not. (This is a good reason for never living at ground or basement level.) Fines are not a myth either, though you'll be treated more leniently if you're a nice middle-class girl who tearfully apologises for having got all confused – a good skill to cultivate.

Decide your house rules for food. Will you share the supermarket bills, in which case you'll be miffed that someone else has used all the communal milk? Or do you keep separate, personalised sections in the fridge and cupboards, in which case you'll be miffed that someone else has used all your milk? The same goes for toilet rolls and washing powder. And powdered milk.

Everyone ignores cleaning rotas so there's little point in setting one up. Similarly, in mixed houses, the girls always end up doing more cleaning than the boys. Male bluffers can make up some theory to explain this, based on 'evolution' ('as hunters, men evolved to be unfazed by blood and dirt, but as child-rearers, women developed better ability to spot germs', etc.), to justify why the bathroom doesn't need cleaning, or does, and why someone else should have to do it. Female bluffers can simply say that they prefer not to live like pigs, delivering the clinching phrase 'with other people's pubic hair', and stomping out of the room. This usually wins it.

Privacy is an issue. Short of physically locking up your stuff, you can't guarantee that curious visiting friends of housemates won't accidentally open your diary, say, when they were innocently seeing if you had a corkscrew under your mattress. Use this to your advantage if there's information you want people to know without telling them yourself – the charity work you don't like to talk about, or somebody you fancy but can't tell them in person.

HEALTHY EATING, AND HOW TO AVOID IT

You'll be an expert on eating out well on the cheap. Not for you the greasy spoon cafés, sickly Chinese takeaways or nauseous kebab vans – not that you admit to, anyway. You can talk confidently about that FE college's catering department nearby, for instance ('It's five-star cuisine and just a fiver for three courses. One of the chefs is apparently going to The Ivy next year…'). And, of course, you've scoured websites for the best-value restaurants, the more ethnic the better ('We found an Albanian/Burmese/Bolivian place. Amazing – really fresh and healthy food and dirt cheap – it's in their culture, you see…').

As for eating in, a fruit bowl in your room gives the impression of getting your five a day. Obviously, you keep it empty, to give the impression you've just eaten the contents. Otherwise people will notice that the bananas are black and the oranges blue. Even if you're doing a still-life module in history of art, it's hard to justify.

To help you eat what you like – instead of what a leaflet (written by an overweight, alcoholic, chain-smoking, failed medic-turned-journalist) tells you – do some internet research. Find some did-you-knows about nutrition and use them to your advantage.

For example, justify fish and chips on the grounds

that it's 'actually healthier than pizza or kebabs'. Canned fruit and orange juice count towards the five a day – but commercially produced smoothies are full of sugar and salt, as you'll point out to anyone drinking one; imply you make your own. And, of course, you can dismiss the whole five-a-day thing as a government myth if you like; again, a web search will provide the answers.

Similar web research can be used to support any viewpoint whatever on food: that vegetarianism/ veganism is far healthier, or else unhealthier, or more moral, or immoral, or more sustainable, or less, than eating meat/vegetarianism; that oily fish is the key to lifelong health, or just to bad breath; that 'chemicals' in food are the cause of all these modern allergies; or that all these modern allergies are just attention-seeking nonsense. Remember: at university, it isn't what you argue, it's how convincingly you argue it.

If cooking yourself, anything can be described as 'curry' or 'ratatouille' depending on what it most resembles at the end. Don't admit that you've just produced a hopeless version of something off a supermarket recipe card: pass it off as an 'old family recipe' or suchlike. Then you can blame your great-grandmother, who never had the chance to go to university and had to leave school at nine.

DOCTORS AND DENTISTS

Register with your university or local doctor's surgery, as well as your GP at home. That way, you can divide your weekly alcohol units between them. Usually people don't bother registering with a dentist in addition to the one at home. That's just as well, given the impossibility of finding NHS dentists these days.

CLOTHES AND HOUSEHOLD WARES

First stop: Primark. For the more ethically motivated, charity shops are also great places to buy cheap clothes and household flotsam and jetsam. Plus you'll fit in with the hipsters who pay far more for similarly worn-looking jumpers from American Apparel. Don't let heated discussions about the difference between morals and ethics distract anybody from your moral/ethical superiority.

FOOD AND DRINK

Almost every supermarket has a line of affordable own-brand basics (even Waitrose). Just look for the brashest two-tone packaging on the shelves. Although the quality as well as the breadth of these lines has improved, it is important to know your basics. For example: basics teabags are great but basics bin bags will break, and basics burgers are horsemeat.

TRAVEL

A young person's railcard (costs £30, gives a third off every ticket) is a must. Being able to preach, 'Oh, but you recoup your money almost instantly' is worth the initial cost itself. Don't flash it around if you have an embarrassing middle name.

IT'S ALL ACADEMIC

READING LISTS

Don't be daunted by reading lists. They were compiled in haste by distracted tutors unsure whether the titles are still, or ever were, in print. To give the impression of familiarity, pick one title – any title – from the 'Further reading' section and read the introduction. It's the oldest trick in the book, but that's fine because a) this isn't school and nobody is trying to catch you out any more, and b) your supervisor will be pleased that you read at least one book, namely the one with the oldest trick listed in it.

The only time you genuinely need to read a book cover to cover is if your supervisor wrote it. It's probably on the list for royalty-boosting purposes rather than relevance, but you will be expected to know it.

Otherwise, talk vaguely about having done 'background reading' and 'reading around the subject'. Anything can be justified this way: will.i.am's as yet unpublished autobiography has valuable insights into British cultural history, for instance; that book about the Premier League season has fascinating information for engineers about goal-line technology, etc.

LECTURERS/TUTORS

Academics – your lecturers, tutors, professors – are your friends. (Unless you go on to do a PhD discrediting all their research, of course.) They will give up a lot of their valuable time and knowledge to help you get the best degree possible. They have to, because all their future funding and job security – 'tenure' – depends on results.

There are five types of academic. Get to know them (but not too closely):

Mentors
The ones who inspire you to get out of bed for a nine o'clock lecture, or to actually go and see that exhibition at the British Museum before it closes. They're fun and engaging and use Hollywood movies to explain complex psychoanalytic theory, or currently viral YouTube parodies to elucidate the finer details of intellectual property law. They do cool, non-academic things during holidays, like take their rock band on a tour of Cuba. Pass marks in their paper will beat the average for the year. If you're in any way attracted to them, they default to the category below.

LILFs, TILFs, SILFs
These are Lecturers/Tutors/Supervisors I'd Like to Fancy.

(Other variants of the acronym exist.) Invariably married with children or gay – whichever is less convenient for you – and not attractive in real terms, this is magnified by their drab surroundings. They do dull things during holidays like redecorate the bedroom, and when they tell you in unnecessary detail about this, you wonder if it's some sort of come-on.

As above, picking their papers will ensure that you do better in your end-of-year exams. Often mistaken for mentors, any work ethic they inspire is aesthetically, not academically, motivated.

Oldies

Wispy white or grey hair; corduroy jackets with mismatching suede elbow patches; leather briefcase; resistance to technology and punctuality; deep-set dislike for the rest of the university administration. Often double up as mentors, but have tenure. Whispered about as hero or idol: 'Apparently he used to be a freedom fighter in South America... she's the world's leading expert on a particular kind of snail,' etc. They do intriguing things during holidays like have former heads of state as house guests. The ultimate bluff is to be seen having a drink with them, preferably a malt whisky or artisan gin.

Mumblers

Not to be confused with oldies, these are the faculty members with absolutely no stage presence, making it irrelevant whether or not they have anything interesting to say. Nobody knows what they do during their holidays as they've never explained it comprehensibly. The only useful thing about a mumbler is that you can legitimately mumble utter rubbish back at them.

Half-wits

Neither inspiring, attractive, endearing nor easy to hoodwink; in other words, few redeeming qualities. Spend their holidays researching their niche subject. Prone to giving too much attention to the annoying know-all who arrives five minutes early and yet saves their question (which they already know the answer to) for the last five minutes of the class. There's a reason for this: they used to be them.

However alike some academics might seem to you, remember you have a huge advantage: students mostly look alike to them, with the same regulation-fashion hairstyles, make-up, clothes, and even selfie poses. Use this to your advantage, taking credit for good things actually done by others, or pretending your misdeeds were actually someone else resembling you. Your tutors, still confusing you with that other one even in your final year, will be too embarrassed to investigate.

LECTURES

The archetypal image of student life: a draughty, high-ceilinged theatre with tiered rows of wooden benches angled towards a professor of something obscure peering through his glasses at the jumble of notes on the lectern in front of him, perhaps talking in Latin, on a sunny afternoon... In reality, you will be watching a PowerPoint presentation projected onto the whitewashed wall of a mostly-empty prefab at half past nine in the morning, finishing early because of a technical problem. Increasingly these days, lectures are available to watch online, live or as catch-up, through some 'virtual learning environment' or similar, so you can miss it from the comfort of your own bed.

If you do attend lectures, work in the offbeats. Every time the rest of the room starts scribbling or typing, recline in your chair and leisurely examine your cuticles. When they're bored and nothing is happening, write intently on your laptop. This is a great way to psych people out (*see* 'Exams', page 99).

For arts students, a more convenient alternative is sourcing TV documentaries and radio podcasts. Louis Theroux's back catalogue is fantastic for anthropology students, for instance. BBC Radio 4's *In Our Time* is an encyclopaedic archive of radio broadcasts that covers everything from Romanticism to the theory of relativity. All of which can be listened to from the comfort of your own bed at an hour to suit you, and it's less embarrassing falling asleep there than in lectures. Though possibly more crowded.

For science students, attendance at lectures is more important. In the arts, only knowing what everyone else knows isn't as impressive as knowing something they don't. In the sciences, though, where understanding is gained in a linear and cumulative way, not knowing what everybody else knows is more likely to result in a medical malpractice suit or a collapsing bridge than a high first. But don't despair. Provided you can stay awake, lectures are the least demanding format in which to consume the expertise of your academic elders. And despite being timetabled for an hour each, they are only 50 minutes long; the idea is to give you time to travel between lectures, though in practice nobody manages two lectures in a row.

Contrary to popular belief, the best excuse for missing a lecture is not a hangover: it's having a cold. No 100-word summary that finally explains postmodernism is worth stifling a cough or plugging a runny nose for 50 minutes. Which may be why nobody quite understands postmodernism.

The lectures most worth attending are the ones just before the exam. The lecturers inevitably realise, in panic, that they've forgotten to cover a question which is about to come up. So watch for the telltale signs: 'I know the timetable said we'd cover Wagner's operas, but instead I'd like to talk a bit about Stravinsky…' That means there's a question on Stravinsky in the exam, and you're just about to get the answer provided on a plate.

If you have to miss an unmissable lecture, there are some recovery tactics. The first is repeated lectures. This is like catch-up TV, except the time delay is a year, not an hour. The freshers won't even recognise each other, and so will assume you're supposed to be there. The second is persuading someone to 'share' their lecture notes with you. This is a bit more of a gamble because other people's notes range from revelatory to incomprehensible. Finally, you might find a recording or transcript of the lecture. These are often uploaded onto the university website to aid dyslexic students. Have no qualms about piggy-backing on resources aimed at others: this is called 'using your initiative' (and they all get free Macs, anyway).

If all else fails, you can always default to JSTOR (that's JournalSTORage, a library of scholarly papers and journals, minus the dust) – useful but time-consuming, and means having to develop genuine research skills – or, as a quick and dirty last resort, Wikipedia. This means having to develop a very good bullshit detector, though this is another vital research skill.

TECHNOLOGY

Your phone will be crammed full of apps. As far as your parents are concerned, these are vital study aids, which is why they bought you the iPhone in the first place. So, to keep up your reputation, scan lists of 'most useful apps for students' online and go on about how useful they are: StudyBlue, Evernote, SoundNote, Office Lens, Timetable, Imindmap, GoConqr, etc. Talk of money and health monitors may impress them too: Splittable (sharing out restaurant bills) and Drinkaware (counting your units, if you're sober enough to operate it), for instance.

Whereas, of course, the apps you actually use on your phone are games, streaming and dating.

As so many apps appear and then disappear when their startup funding is blown, you can make up anything to sound tech-savvy to fellow students, perhaps with a missing 'e' near the end, without fear of being rumbled. ('Yes, RefME's ability to create citations from scanning a book's barcode is OK. But I use RefMakr, which is miles better. Sadly you can't download it any more, and it's copy-protected...')

You can spook any tutor by making out that the technology they use is obsolete, slow and uncool, and so by implication they are too. ('Wordpress? That's a bit old-fashioned. Facebook? I think my mum's on it. Email? Oh yeah, my nan uses that...' etc.)

ESSAYS

Science students can skip this section. The longest sentence demanded of you – apart from the suspended one you receive after that drunken business with the shopping trolley – is the equation for standard model Lagrangian density. (But then this does code the theory of everything, except for gravitons, and not even *War and Peace* covers gravitons.)

> The most important thing about essays is the obvious: read the question, and then answer it.

The most important thing about essays is the obvious: read the question, and then answer it. It will be straightforward. Essays are designed to show what you do know, not what you don't. So, find a way of applying what you know, or at least what you've cut and pasted from someone's website, to the question. Some things can be applied universally – arguments over the difference between morals and ethics, for instance.

The more footnotes[1] you can put in an essay, the better. So long as they appear plausible sources, nobody will ever check them out[2]. Said to have been invented by the Venerable Bede[3], they're vital but can also be an Achilles heel[4]. The American feminist and writer Joanna Russ recalls asking 'a young dissertation writer whether her suddenly grayed hair was due to ill health or personal tragedy; she answered: "It was the footnotes."'[5] Increase your footnote count with judicious use of 'ibid'[6] and 'passim'[7].

Luckily, most academic texts have migrated online, which means that with a quick CTRL+F search you can look up that passage, on which page it was, in the journal by the guy with the hair, you know the one.

Essay-writing services abound on the internet, despite talk of shutting them down, though they're actually used far less than newspapers might have your parents believe.

[1] Like this.

[2] Anon, *Big Book of Facts*.

[3] http://www.ship-of-fools.com/mystery/2008/1594.html

[4] Ovid, *Metamorphoses*.

[5] Russ, J (1983). *How to Suppress Women's Writing*.

[6] Ibid.

[7] Ainsley, R (1988). *The Bluffer's Guide to University* (1st ed.) passim.

For a few quid, the online outfits promise you a top-quality, bespoke piece of academic work. You know better. The writer will be a failed hack escaping creditors on a narrowboat, or a failed academic with English as a third language.

Mention the example of Sheffield Eng Lit student Dan Burns. In 2018, with the collusion of his tutor, he bought such an essay on Victorian literature for £65, as a journalistic exercise. It was terribly written, riddled with errors, and would have got a third. As you tell this story, watch for the nervous guilty glances of those who've been tempted by such things.

(Of course, if you really want to catch someone out, tell them essay-writing services are a really good idea and they should buy one immediately.)

TUTORIALS AND SEMINARS

The only difference between tutorials and seminars is the number of people in attendance: from fewer than there should be in seminars down to hardly anyone in tutorials. In these classes you'll be expected to discuss the things that you've written in relation to the things that people most probably far cleverer than you have written. Don't think that unpacking your own opinions will be any easier than explaining somebody else's. In your defence, academics tend to have the added advantage of knowing what on earth it is they're on about. In your defence again, they're notoriously bad at imparting this expertise. So if asked to feed back on Sir Philip Sidney's *The Defence of Poesy* or another equally esoteric text, defer to the most elaborate bluff of all: no bluff. Saying that you have absolutely no idea what Pavlov was trying to prove with his dogs or what Plato was trying to illustrate with all those rings will no doubt be the most refreshing contribution your supervisor has heard all year and will, hopefully, ignite his or her own latent dislike for the great thinkers.

If this tactic returns a disappointed sigh, then change tack and interrogate the terms of the question instead (*see* 'Interviews', page 28, and 'Essays', page 94). This is easy. All you need to do is repeat the sentence you've just been asked with a randomly chosen emphasis:

Supervisor 'James, how would you describe the developing role of feminism in today's society?'

You 'The *developing* role of feminism in today's society?' (Or, 'The developing role of feminism in *today's* society?', etc.)

But beware: play the language trickster and you may encourage people to try to catch you out. If you refer to Daniel Defoe's cockney heroine *Moll Flanders,* for example, as being 'literally a bag of money or a jewel dropped on the highway', this may elicit a response such as, 'I didn't know Defoe was interested in abiogenesis.' This sort of semantic nonsense can go on forever.

THE LIBRARY
Vast rooms, infrequently visited, full of little-borrowed old

books and shiny new PCs – and still the university hasn't quite worked out what the balance should be. With Wi-Fi in your room and a university website login, there may be no reason to enter a library until final exams – to at least adopt the appearance of hard work, or because the library will have become a bit of a social hub.

Choose your station carefully. Near, but not next to, the toilet is best, depending on how many free refill coffees you had in the café opposite. Levels of visibility are also tricky to get right. Opt for a seat in full view of the main thoroughfare, or in the most secluded corner possible – never anywhere in between; you'll only get cramp from craning your neck at the sound of every pair of passing footsteps.

Once you've found the seat, become parochial. Don't worry if your set of unopened highlighters spends more time saving this seat than you do sitting in it; everybody marks their territory out in this way. If you don't, you'll be forced to play the part of *flâneur*, aimlessly wandering the library's many floors looking for bed and board. But even this is better than sitting at home – the more hours you clock in the library (working or otherwise), the better your exam results, allegedly.

When you do sit down to work, study effectively. Declaring yourself to be 'a visual learner' and constructing elaborately colour-coded spider diagrams not only means you have more pens and paper to fill your section of the table with, but will also throw off the other lacklustre revision strategies of other students. (They only award a certain percentage of firsts every year. Just saying.)

Despite the introduction of Wi-Fi and vending machines, librarians remain traditional in their attitudes to noise. That means headphones, silenced phones and whispers are a must. But rather than being a pain, these stipulations allow you to mask what you're really listening to.

EXAMS

Exams are all that stand between you and genius status. There's a surprisingly generous crumple zone for failure: 40% is the standard pass rate; half-marks guarantee you a 2:2 (aka a 'Desmond' – Tutu, after the South African archbishop and activist), 60% will get you a 2:1 and 70% or over means a first, or 'Geoff' (Hurst, as in the footballer). Firsts are getting easier and easier to come by. In 2013, 20% of UK graduates got one, but in 2018 this had risen to 28%. Grade inflation has been going a long time: Cambridge awarded firsts to only 10% of students in 1960, but in 2018 the figure had reached 32%.

Use such figures to prove that standards are getting better ('universities are getting more results-focused, like every other modern business... in the days of grants students didn't have much incentive to study hard... growth of firsts is helped by hard-working overseas students from Asia') or worse ('universities are cooking the figures, like every other modern business... students paying £9,000 a year expect to be able to buy a first... growth of firsts is all in arts subjects, proof of grade inflation.'). So, while getting a Geoff might not impress employers these day quite as much as your family, it's nevertheless attainable and worth going for in those final exams. Here's how:

1. Read the directions all the way through before beginning.

2. Have a banana before you go in to prevent your stomach embarrassing you out of hunger and sip water throughout; apparently both will increase your productivity.

3. Don't panic and quote lines from films or TV as philosophical platitudes. However culturally clueless your examiner is, they will know that it was Spiderman and not Voltaire who most recently said, 'With great power comes great responsibility.'

4. If you do have the perfect quote but no idea who said it, attribute it to Karl Marx, *Das Kapital* (1867): nobody has ever finished it so won't be able to prove you wrong.

5. Raise your hand in the first five minutes, and every half-hour thereafter, to ask for extra paper. This is guaranteed to psych out those in your near vicinity, decreasing the average mark in your year and subsequently increasing your chances of graduating in the top percentile.

6. Use your handwriting to disguise your spelling or fumbled equations. If you're typing your exam script, pray that spell check has been left enabled.

7. If you run out of time, bullet points are more permissible than you might think. Examiners are surprisingly sympathetic to this last-ditch attempt at imparting your knowledge. This is almost certainly because shorthand lists are infinitely easier to read than the essays of students who realise that they've finished with five minutes to spare and return to riddle their work with arrows and numbers.

8. Do quote Terry Pratchett, who once wrote: 'It is very important to be sober when you take an exam. Many worthwhile careers in the street-cleansing, fruit-picking and subway-guitar-playing industries have been founded on a lack of understanding of this simple fact.'

9. Ignore numbers 2 through 8 and go to the pub.[8]

Exams, like this chapter, can seem like a prescriptive litany of dos and don'ts. If this doesn't sit well with your pink streak of hair, political dogma or general outlook on life and bluffing, which it more than likely doesn't, remember that rules are there to be broken and examiners will always appreciate being shocked out of their slumber. The myth of the student who simply wrote, 'This is,' in response to the question, 'Define courage', is the ultimate accolade for the student of bluffing. (If you can convince someone that this ever actually happened, your bluffing prowess is proven.)

---

[8]Just kidding.

But remember: for it to be clever you have to have got there first. As Christopher Columbus once said, there are no prizes for coming second, or for rediscovering America. Or was that Marx in *Das Kapital*? (Actually, what Columbus said was 'Where the hell are we now?') Either way, remember that Carol Vorderman got a third (or a 'Douglas', as in 'Hurd', the former foreign secretary) and still went on to be a successful TV presenter, or that Paul Whitehouse dropped out completely and became a high-flying comedian.

REVISION TECHNIQUES

Obviously, there's only one effective way to revise, and that's to read, understand, write a lot of notes, and practise. But that shouldn't stop you from talking about 'miracle' techniques that make it all easy. Singing important quotes or formulas, for example, or 'assisting your memory' with scented candles, or acting things out in the style of Shakespeare or Pinter. They're unlikely to work, but make great entertainment.

FURTHER EDUCATION, MINIMUM WORK

If you want to extend your student experience after getting a degree, there are many options for avoiding responsibility and proper work for a while longer.

The following assumes full-time postgraduate study. Part-time options for all exist, usually doubling the amount of time involved, often suitable for those with proper jobs. You probably won't meet any such students as they'll be too busy; you'll only ever see them arriving ten minutes late for lectures and then rushing off at the end.

MASTER'S

This is the most obvious way to delay entry into the real world: one add-on year of study.

Plausible excuses for doing your master's are to 'enhance your CV' and improve your 'job opportunities'. The extra year of 'study' in fact consists of more student loans, party-chasing, house-sharing and getting every student discount you can. It will be a prescribed course, with some mildly impressive but flimsy hint of speciality. There will be scheduled lectures and so on, most of which you will end up attending because you are, after all, a serious academic. On the other hand, with most of your contemporaries now in gainful employment, you probably failed to find where the party was last night.

On passing it, your BA or BSc will be augmented by an MA or MSc or similar. The promise of these letters, and the word 'master's', are usually enough to convince parents or sponsors to provide further financial subsidy.

Bear in mind that if you've had the good sense to do your arts degree at one of the ancient universities of Scotland – Aberdeen, Dundee, Edinburgh, Glasgow and St Andrews – you are automatically awarded an MA Hons. Unless of course, you are awarded an MA Ord (short for 'Ordinary') which takes three years as opposed to four but doesn't sound quite as good. (NB: Bluffers should know that although Dundee didn't receive its Royal Charter until 1967, it qualifies as one of the 'ancients' as a former college of St Andrews.)

Note that if you have an Oxford or Cambridge degree, you can apply for an MA a few years after graduating without any further study simply by sending off a small admin fee of £10 or so. Never, therefore, be overawed by the legend 'MA (Oxon)' or 'MA (Cantab)' on someone's business card. They simply sent off a cheque to obtain it, instead of putting in hours of laborious effort house-sharing, partying and capitalising on cheap rail fares.

PGCE

Postgraduate certificate in education: a one-year course qualifying you as a schoolteacher, consisting of learning modules and a lot of teaching practice in real schools. As the joke goes, 'Those who can, do; those who can't, teach; those who can't teach, teach teachers.'

There's a stereotypical view of teachers complaining to their friends in other jobs about misconceptions of 'school holidays' (wearily pointing out that it's the pupils who get the time off, not the teachers, who have admin work through it all).

This stereotype isn't universally true. Most teachers are too busy doing term-time admin, marking and lesson plans to spend any time seeing their friends at all. Job prospects with a PGCE are good, though, especially in maths and science, where there's a dire shortage of teachers. After your chaotic teaching practice terms, and your first year at an inner-city comprehensive trying to interest kids in Pythagoras's Theorem, you'll quickly appreciate why.

PhD, OR 'DOCTORATE'

The next big thing after your degree: nominally three years, in practice up to seven, of original research that enables you to call yourself 'doctor'.

This, at the very least, means that when people at parties think you're a medic and ask about their dodgy knee, you can ask them to take all their clothes off. Of course, you are not a medical doctor, but a doctor of philosophy (PhD and DPhil both signify this, whatever the arcane subject you actually researched).

A PhD usually starts out as an MPhil (Master of Philosophy), and gets upgraded after a year, which gives you a get-out if 'things don't work out'.

Indeed, abandoned PhDs are common. Famous examples to cite, if you have to do this, include American economist Alan Greenspan (dropped out of his economics PhD because of lack of money); singer Art Garfunkel (dropped out of maths PhD); satirist Armando Iannucci (dropped out of PhD on John Milton); and 'Queen' guitarist Brian May (dropped out of astronomy PhD for a rock career, but completed it over 30 years later).

Your PhD thesis, probably the length of a phone book and roughly as interesting to the layman, will likely only ever be read by five people.

The 'doctor' concept is said to have originated in twelfth-century Bologna, but the PhD itself is generally attributed to William von Humboldt at the University of Berlin in the early 1800s. The idea took off in the USA; the first American PhD, in 1861, was only six pages long, on the theme of brevity in art. Nowadays that's the length of the title of many a thesis.

The title of your thesis
...is both vital (as it defines every word you write for several years) and trivial (because nobody apart from

you, your supervisor and your assessors will have a clue what it means). You will get wearily used to answering the question, 'What is your PhD about, then?' with the title of your thesis receiving a bewildered silence and killing the dinner-party conversation stone dead.

Funding
The most thorough research you will do in your entire doctorate is trying to locate funding. There are essentially two ways to get a place to do a PhD.

The first (often in something interesting such as arts or humanities) is relatively easy but expensive; you pitch a proposal yourself to a university which, desperate for your business, says this is a brilliant idea. You then spend six months online trying in vain to get a grant before deciding to work flipping burgers and doing it part-time.

The second (often in something important but dull, such as lab-based science research) is much more secure but unusual; someone approaches you with a pre-packaged project, making you more of a research assistant.

Either way, your PhD will involve working under a supervisor. The choice of supervisor is vital, for it is they who guide you through the entire three (i.e., seven) years. They shape your final thesis, and are the only people you can possibly blame if it goes wrong.

There are no set guidelines or qualification standard to determine whether you 'pass' at the end. Your PhD thesis, probably the length of a phone book and roughly as interesting to the layman, will likely only ever be read by five people. These are: you, your supervisor, your secondary supervisor and the two assessors at the end. You can choose these last two, so choose wisely.

POST-DOCTORAL RESEARCH

There's a whole, rarefied, world beyond even the PhD: that of post-docs and second-post-docs. This is remote territory, where specifying the title of your post-doc thesis produces a bewildered silence even from PhD students, and kills even faculty water-cooler conversations stone dead.

ACADEMIC HIERARCHY

If during all this research you become good enough doing the round of conferences, undergraduate teaching and lecturing, book reviews that only other PhD candidates ever read, and schmoozing at departmental parties, then with luck you can bluff your way through academia forever.

Below is the hierarchy of university positions, increasing in order of eminence. The better you are at bluffing, the further up you can aim:

dropout
undergraduate
diploma student
master's student
PhD student
research assistant
research fellow
lecturer

senior lecturer
reader
professor
vice chancellor
TV personality

OTHER STUDY

The Erasmus scheme aims to let students spend three months of their course at an equivalent university on the Continent, without paying extra tuition fees. (Its post-Brexit status is unclear, and will be for some time – like most things involved in leaving the EU.) In practice, students from Britain seem reluctant to engage with the rest of Europe, perhaps because of language difficulties; the UK receives twice as many Erasmus participants as it sends out.

So you don't have much to live up to. Merely by showing an interest in the scheme – and perhaps 'being gutted' when you are unable to get a place because of some imagined technicality – you can bolster your credibility as an internationally minded citizen of the world.

U3A (UNIVERSITY OF THE THIRD AGE)

Not a university, but a network of self-managed local cooperatives of people no longer in full-time employment who give learning sessions in their homes. There are small registration but not tuition fees.

'Lectures' can be on anything from learning German to making beer to playing the ukulele, or even all three at once, so it's no wonder they have some very enthusiastic devotees. The typical U3A devotee is a retired professional, though as jobs become scarcer the 'no longer in full-time employment' demographic may shift down in age dramatically.

MORE GAP YEARS

With employment far from guaranteed on completion of your degree or postgrad work, it's perfectly legitimate to continue dodging the real world by simply taking another gap year.

Here, you can do everything you enjoyed from your first gap year over again, and avoid anything you didn't, but claim more 'maturity' and 'understanding' in your continued 'experience'.

Justify anything you do by stressing the 'employability skills' you are gaining, especially buzzwords such as 'teamwork', 'immersion', 'engagement' and 'responsibility', which are more important now than in your pre-degree gap year.

For instance, booking a group train ticket and a hostel dorm online for you and three backpackers you hooked up with in Sydney becomes 'organised cultural exchange visit in Australasia; responsible for planning itinerary and all travel and accommodation arrangements for large group'.

Similarly, getting retweeted by organisation X, however niche, becomes 'worked on publicity campaign team for X, liaising with press and social media department over most effective marketing strategies, bringing message to over 25,000 Twitter followers'.

PhDs WITHOUT WORK

Various scam emails promise to 'award a PhD' in return for a PayPal transfer, rather than any genuine study. These come, of course, from non-accredited organisations. You wouldn't expect Oxbridge to give you postgraduate qualifications simply by sending a cheque. Of course you wouldn't.

Save your money. If you want a bogus title, you don't have to pay anyone anything. You can simply call yourself 'doctor' – or, indeed, anything you like – so long as it's not done dishonestly or to defraud.

The whole dodgy doctorate business came to light in 2006 with Paul McKenna, a TV hypnotist and self-help author. A columnist alleged that McKenna's PhD, awarded by post through a non-accredited organisation for a 50,000-word thesis that became a book, was bogus. In the ensuing libel case, the judge sided with the hypnotist; while the PhD might be academically flimsy, he said, McKenna sincerely believed in the validity of his work, and so the criticism of him was libellous.

DROPPING OUT/CHANGING DIRECTION

Around 30,000 students a year never finish their course, either because they drop out, finish earlier with a lesser degree, or change to something else.

If this happens to you, there are several positive spins to put on it. Your school pushed you onto a wholly inappropriate course, for instance, but thanks to you it has realised its mistake and you have generously saved other students from the same fate. You have learned a great deal about yourself. You now realise, usefully, what your true calling is, and can switch course with confidence.

Present it to employers as a triumph of self-discovery and adaptability, rather than a good excuse to start the whole student thing over again with an even higher overdraft.

Worried parents financing your incomplete studies should be given soothing examples of dropouts who became multibillionaires, such as Microsoft's Bill Gates or Facebook's Mark Zuckerberg (both enrolled at Harvard but left before graduating) or Apple's Steve Jobs (abandoned 'studies' at Portland's Reed College after six months). Use them to justify the fact that you spent so much of term time playing computer games.

INFORMAL STUDY

If you end up doing nothing for a while after your degree, dress this up as 'informal study', with vague references to 'lifelong learning'.

For instance, you're not just sitting at home playing guitar, but 'taking lessons' (which actually consist of watching YouTube clips).

Cultivate relationships with foreign language speakers. Then you can pass off picking up your takeaway, for example, as 'studying Chinese' in a 'language exchange'.

If all else fails, claim to be 'writing a book' supposedly based on something you 'researched' as an obscure part of your degree.

WORK-LIFE BALANCE

GOING BACK HOME

After your degree, things can come down to earth with a bump. In today's 'boomerang generation', more UK graduates than ever are returning to live with their parents on finishing their course, usually because of finances.

So, should this happen, portray it as a positive. It's the new norm, the new smart way. Make out it is a win-win for both you and your parents. In fact, imply you're largely doing it to please them: they 'love having you back', or perhaps you're 'house-sitting' for them while they spend six semi-retired months in South America.

Appear active; web surfing can be represented as 'applying for jobs', which is why you spend so much time on the internet. Doing something vaguely useful-sounding such as 'working on my Spanish' (hanging out in a tapas bar) or 'doing business studies online' (watching *The Apprentice* on BBC iPlayer) gives the appearance of being fully occupied.

To the public, and especially parents, compare your situation favourably with that of vague 'friends from uni' who are now working in London. You are 'saving for a deposit on a flat'; they are getting deeper in debt, thanks to exorbitant rents and season tickets.

GETTING A JOB

Getting a job is a zero-sum game at first: what money you earn is swallowed by rent, transport, bills and student loan repayments, and you may look back on your years of 'hardship' at uni with nostalgia. Nevertheless, it may have to be done, partly to reassure parents and friends that you are not merely drifting (i.e., enjoying yourself), but mainly to reassure future employers that you are following a methodical and ambitious career plan.

Around 400,000 students graduate every year, and they'll all be applying for the same job as you, along with most of the other 14 million graduates living in the UK. Or so it'll feel. With an average 46 applicants for every graduate position, and some organisations attracting 160 applicants per post, you will have to use bluffing skills more effectively than ever to get a job.

GETTING WORK EXPERIENCE

It's hard to get a job without experience: roughly a third of all graduate positions go to someone who's already worked for the hiring company or done the same sort of work. It's a bit like getting a loan by proving you don't need one: you can only get a first job if you can show that you've had one already. You don't need to be an English grad to spot the catch-22.

Work experience, therefore, is key to getting a job these days. And many firms offer such opportunities, in three types:

Shadowing
What it is Following someone around for a few days or weeks as an unpaid observer.
What actually happens See how inefficient most offices are. Hear shadowee moan about how busy they are and why nothing is their fault. You get chatted up by someone who confides about wanting to leave.
How you represent it in job interviews Valuable insight into business. Sat in on important meetings. Saw first-hand how decisions are made. Maintained close working relationships with colleagues.

Internship
What it is One to three months or so, often in your holiday time, of being a paid, or more often unpaid, member of some project or team.
What actually happens Though they looked forward to 'having your help', your team are too busy to explain the intricacies of their work, and simply do it themselves. You get shooed aside to do photocopying, make tea, order stationery, etc. Any token creative work you do – the Twitter feed, or redesigning a company intranet page, perhaps – is blocked by some group of people you never meet. You get chatted up by someone who confides about wanting to leave.

How you represent it in job interviews Valuable insight into business. Took responsibility for a wide range of tasks. Helped set strategies for social media. Maintained close working relationships with colleagues.

Placements
What it is Six to 12 months of paid work with the intention of it leading to a permanent post.
What actually happens You get solid work experience, but only after you've spent the first three months waiting for the ID card and codes needed to get in and out, access the internet, use the toilet, etc., thus doing nothing for the first half of your placement and then too much for the second half. You get chatted up by someone who confides that the post you're supposed to be in line for is actually going to be axed.
How you represent it in job interviews Valuable insight into business. Coped with deadlines, multitasked, worked on several simultaneous projects. Maintained close working relationships with employment law solicitors.

UNDERSTANDING JOB ADVERTS

Never take a job advert at face value. For instance, one requiring candidates who 'think outside the box' is not looking for originality. They are looking for plodders who can express themselves only in buzzwords and clichés such as 'think outside the box'.

Here is a list of other buzzwords, and their real meanings:

Fast-moving People leave after three weeks.

Lively, bustling Chaotic.

Exciting, prestigious Badly paid.

Competitive salary As bad as everyone else's.

Great perks Badly paid.

Vital work Boring.

Sleek, modern offices Beyond the ring road with no public transport.

City-centre offices Cramped and noisy, up seven flights of stairs.

Urgently required Previous post holder left in tears after three weeks.

Maternity cover She'll still try to be in control.

Following a promotion He'll still try to be in control.

You must...

...be a multitasker. We're disorganised.

...be a self-starter. Your manager is useless.

...take on responsibility quickly with the same salary (and be prepared to take the blame).

THE CV

There are any number of example CVs available online, many of them directly contradictory. Perhaps the best option is to find a friend who actually managed to get a job similar to the one you want, and mimic theirs.

Be careful that you don't cut and paste too specifically, or you might end up unintentionally including inaccurate information about you. This is to be avoided. Your CV should only contain intentionally inaccurate information.

LINKEDIN, FACEBOOK, ETC.

Create a LinkedIn profile which lists your skills in detail, or at least the skills you wish you had. Ideally, have a look at people in a position you'd like to be in and learn from how they present themselves. You'll never actually get any work or job offers from it, but it creates a good rapport with people LinkingIn, and sounds good.

It's a good idea to have a sensible email address for job applications; ciderhead@shagfest.com may not convey a 'professional' image.

As for your Facebook profile, this is where you can really express yourself. Put up your holiday pictures, banter with friends and show your true character to the world.

Therefore never, ever do it under your own name, or in any way that an employer, police officer, partner or any member of the public might trace.

It's a good idea to have a sensible email address for job applications and professional use only; ciderhead@ shagfest.com, for example, may not convey a 'professional' image, unless of course you're applying to a video games company.

THE APPLICATION FORM

Many companies now have compulsory online application forms. All are badly designed and take hours to fill in. It's a good idea to have a text file somewhere with details of your previous jobs, academic record, exaggerations about your achievements, etc., expressed in various ways, so you can cut and paste. There's little positive you can say about online application forms except that they hardly get read anyway. At least it gives a plausible reason for needing unlimited broadband.

Usually you hear nothing from them ever again. If you're lucky, and there's something they happened to like about you as they fast-forwarded through the 5,000 applications – usually a random factor such as you happen to come from the same town as their partner – you might get an interview.

THE JOB INTERVIEW

You take a train somewhere awful and arrive two hours early, filling the time in with cups of tea in reception and trying to find something interesting in the company newsletter.

You eventually get called in and spend half an hour with someone who's leaving and doesn't really care, and an HR person who has no idea what the job involves and so is looking for someone just like them.

In an interview, you're not judged on how good you might be at the job. You're judged on how good an interviewee you are.

Interviewers rarely set you a task or test of your abilities, though there might be some sort of bogus 'psychometric' personality test they got off the internet. They'll justify this by saying it works, because the candidate with the best score always gets the job, which proves it. English grads will recognise this as a classic case of 'begging the question'. Maths grads with a background in logic will recognise this as a classic case of 'bollocks'.

What to do in interviews
The key is, don't be yourself. Be the person they want you to be. Whatever the work entails, describe yourself as a team player, conscientious but flexible, able to multi-task, a good communicator and, of course, with excellent written English.

Mid-smart but comfortable is probably the best dress code, because the HR person will be in a suit while the other one could be in shorts and T-shirt, so if you're at the casual or too-smart end of the spectrum, you'll get looked up and down by one of them.

First impressions are vital: offer a firm handshake

(but if you hear their knuckles crack, you've gone too far), maintain steady eye-contact, wait to be asked to sit down, don't fiddle with your hair, and ensure that your fingernails are relatively clean.

Prior research on the company and the market is always a good idea. It gives you plenty of intelligent-sounding questions to ask about their challenges, future direction, etc., and hence leaves less time to fill trying to think of Examples Where You Showed Initiative.

At the end of the interview, which has been all smiles and reassuring nods, you'll think the job is yours. The interviewers will assure you that they'll let you know by the end of the week, or Monday at the very latest.

You then won't hear from them for three weeks, at which point you phone to ask. You'll be told by a curt PA that the position has been filled, and 'can I help you with anything else?'

The sheer unpleasant truth is that there aren't nearly enough jobs for all the applicants. Most people end up disappointed. So, if all this happens, you have to turn it to your advantage, if only to reassure parents and friends. The mere fact that you got an interview is positive. Make up some finishing order: you were 'second' out of the 12 interviewees – what a near miss, that's encouraging; or you were 'shortlisted' to the last two, but the boss's god-daughter got the job (as she was always going to).

By all means, you can try asking for feedback about why you didn't get the post, but this is rarely useful. You just get a vague 'very good but another candidate had stronger skills in some areas' kind of answer.

With so many applicants, every way of thinning them down imaginable is used, so you can plausibly cite some random and unfair fact as the cause of your non-appointment ('the HR person said their ex came from the same place as me, and I knew right then…').

Then it's back to the next application.

NEW HOUSE, NEW LIFE

If and when you get that job, you can then become fully independent and your own person at last. You'll probably move into a shared house near the job.

This will be a professional house rather than a student house. It is similar in many ways, such as the fact that nobody admits to having blocked the toilet, everyone ignores the cleaning rota and your milk keeps disappearing. But it has the added stress of everyone having to get up for work. This creates competition for resources in the morning, especially the queue for the loo.

On the plus side, young-professional house parties are much more interesting than student house parties, even if you'll quickly tire of the My Awful Boss conversation.

After a few months, things will settle down and be a bit dull and predictable, so your education is complete. Now you know about life. You can then consider settling down with someone and perhaps even starting a family, for which enormity no amount of training can prepare you.

ß

There's no point in pretending that you know everything about university – nobody does – but if you've got this far and absorbed at least a modicum of the information and advice contained within these pages, then you will almost certainly know more than 99% of the rest of the human race about what it is, why it is, what it's for, and how to make the best use of the next three or four years of dreaming spires and subsidised drinking.

What you now do with this information is up to you, but here's a suggestion: be confident about your newfound knowledge, see how far it takes you, but above all have fun using it. You are now a bona fide expert in the art of bluffing about a stage in life which will help to prepare you for the arduous years of toil which lie ahead. And to reinforce the (paraphrased) refrain of Ol' Blue Eyes: 'If you can bluff it there, you really can bluff it anywhere.'

GLOSSARY

Admissions office University department responsible for admitting the loss of your application.

AHRC (Arts & Humanities Research Council) Body that won't have the money to fund your arts or humanities PhD.

Alumni Former students, usually rich or famous ones cited in publicity, who therefore certainly didn't do Latin (alumnus alumna alumnum alumni alumnae alumna).

BA (Bachelor of Arts) Letters you can put after your name upon completing your degree; marginally better than 'AA'.

BSc Same but for science subjects; also known as 'lab rat'.

Bursary Money to help with living and tuition, awarded on merit (by university) or emotional blackmail (by parents).

Campus Area of concentration of university buildings, except in the lecture halls where nobody's concentrating.

Clearing Equivalent of laterooms.com for university places; also, a place where dead wood has been cut out.

CV At-a-glance guide to why someone should employ you. From Latin *curriculum vitae,* or 'pack of lies'.

Dissertation Written work of several thousand words, usually completed in final year of study, usually about half an hour before the deadline, often borrowed from Wikipedia.

Distance learning Courses with web-based element enabling you to study at a great distance, such as at the back of a new university lecture theatre.

Finals Last, make-or-break exams, whose contents are revealed with heavy hints in immediately preceding lectures by tutors who forgot to cover the topic earlier.

Freshers Bewildered, permanently hungover students beginning first few weeks.

Freshers' week First week of bewildering introductory events.

Graduate Someone with a degree and possibly a job, except among PhDs, when it's someone who only has a degree.

Graduation Scroll-on, scroll-off ceremony.

Grant (archaic) Money you used to get for being a student.

Halls (of residence) Accommodation run by the university, and run down by the students.

Honours (Hons) 'Normal' degree; substandard performance may be dishonourable.

Joint Honours Degree for those who do two things by halves.

Lecture Where lecturers drop unsubtle hints about what's in the exam; therefore sometimes useful to attend.

MA/MSc (Master of Arts/Science) Next step up from a BA/BSc; women, too, are 'masters', not 'mistresses'.

MPhil (Master of Philosophy) Next up from MA/MSc, lower than PhD; for both arts and science, and people not called Phil.

NUS (National Union of Students) Provides support and services; hard to tell when they've organised a strike.

NUS card Discount card that enables you to spend even more of someone else's money.

PhD (Doctor of Philosophy) Postgraduate degree in any subject involving thesis and extensive research, most of it into getting funded.

Prospectus Slick brochure or website persuading you to come to college or university. From Latin for 'look out'.

Rag Week Excuse for semi-intoxicated students to stagger around university towns in fancy dress, harassing innocent passers-by for charitable donations.

Sabbatical Year off to do other stuff; a kind of in-degree (or in-job) gap year.

Sandwich course Degree involving a year or so of work experience eating cheaply.

Semester Half-year; 5% of your work is done in the first semester and 95% in the second, before the exam.

Seminar Teaching class with audience participation.

Term One-third of a year; 2% of your work is done in the first term, 3% in the second and 95% in the third, before the exam.

Tutors Subject supervisors who overlook your work, and hopefully your misdemeanours too.

Tutorial Small group discussion with tutor, hence testing your bluffing powers to the max.

Ucas (Universities and Colleges Admissions Service) Matchmaker for students and universities; also stands for Unduly Confusing, Agonisingly Slow.

Undergraduate Degree student who doesn't have to repay any loans yet.

Vac Holiday; or, (rare) 'vacuum cleaner', aka unused device in student houses.

A BIT MORE BLUFFING...

Bluffer's GUIDE TO BREXIT

Bluffer's GUIDE TO CRICKET

Bluffer's GUIDE TO MANAGEMENT

Bluffer's GUIDE TO CYCLING

Bluffer's GUIDE TO SOCIAL MEDIA

Bluffer's GUIDE TO ETIQUETTE

Bluffer's GUIDE TO RACING

Bluffer's GUIDE TO GOLF

Bluffer's GUIDE TO WINE

Bluffer's GUIDE TO JAZZ

Bluffer's GUIDE TO DOGS

Bluffer's GUIDE TO FISHING

Bluffer's GUIDE TO OPERA

Bluffer's GUIDE TO CHOCOLATE

Bluffer's GUIDE TO CATS

Bluffer's GUIDE TO BEER

Bluffer's GUIDE TO QUANTUM UNIVERSE

Bluffer's GUIDE TO FOOTBALL

Bluffer's GUIDE TO RUGBY

Bluffer's GUIDE TO SKIING

Bluffer's GUIDE TO SEX

Bluffer's GUIDE TO HOLLYWOOD

Bluffer's GUIDE TO POETRY

Bluffer's GUIDE TO JOURNALISM

Bluffer's GUIDE TO PUBLIC RELATIONS

Bluffer's GUIDE TO FORMULA 1

Bluffer's GUIDE TO SURFING

Bluffer's GUIDE TO HIKING

Bluffer's GUIDE TO TENNIS

Bluffer's GUIDE TO UNIVERSITY

Bluffer's GUIDE TO CARS

Available from all good bookshops

bluffers.com